Praise for *Break Your Own Rules*

"Upheavals abound that challenge organizations deeply every day. The interplay of shifting demographics, new technologies, and economic forces is non-stop—and powerful. What does this mean to women who want to change the face of leadership and share power at the top? You need smart, fast help from trusted leadership experts who understand the path from the inside out. You'll get just that in *Break Your Own Rules* by authors Flynn, Heath, and Holt. Its fresh stories, in-depth research, and resonant advice will help you navigate today's real hurdles and drive your career to the highest levels. I look forward to the day when the senior ranks reflect a full 50% of the talent pool, thanks in part to this immensely practical new book."

> —Tammy Erickson, award-winning advisor on engaged organizations; bestselling author of *Workforce Crisis* and *What's Next, Gen X?*

"In the game of business, you've got to know the rules to get ahead. But if you're a woman, there's more: you need to recognize the patterns that continue to hold us back, then you must start practicing 'the new rules of leadership.' Flynn, Heath, and Holt deliver it all in *Break Your Own Rules*. The book is packed with untold stories from the authors' own lives as senior executives, from their current work as leadership coaches to women in Fortune 1000 companies, and from women CEOs across industries. It includes the six road-tested 'new rules' that get women to the top. If your goal is to achieve your highest potential, you'll need this book. It comes with my highest recommendation."

> —Gail Evans, executive VP at CNN (retired); bestselling author of *Play Like a Man, Win Like a Woman*

"Great leadership is by definition uncommon and unconventional. If it were not, most every leader would be great. *Break Your Own Rules* is a provocative yet pragmatic blueprint for ways to reconstruct the models, myths, and molds that restrict leader greatness. It will open your eyes, renovate your mind, and unleash your talent."

> —Chip R. Bell, author of *Wired and Dangerous*

"In our world of unprecedented change, how do organizations become more effective, decisive, and profitable? By having the very best leaders at the top. It's time for women everywhere to break their own rules and start joining the senior ranks in greater numbers. Here's how: buy a copy of this breakthrough book for yourself, and one for a colleague."

> —Charlene Li, founder of Altimeter Group; author of the
> bestselling *Open Leadership*

"Vast numbers of women move business forward every day—yet astonishingly few hold top leadership positions. *Break your Own Rules* addresses this age-old problem in a powerful new way through six specific practices. This book is for every woman, in any industry, who is ready to start engineering her own 'path to power.'"

> —Douglas R. Conant, CEO of Campbell Soup Company;
> coauthor of the bestselling *TouchPoints: Creating Powerful
> Leadership Connections in the Smallest of Moments*

"*Break Your Own Rules* is an unusually fresh, engaging, and tactical book for women who want to fulfill their leadership potential. It's also perfect for men who want the very best people in power. Get your copy today."

> —Mary Matalin, political consultant, commentator, and author

"Over the years and across a few generations, I have had the privilege of participating in American public life in so many ways—as a daughter, wife, mother, and grandmother. As a government servant at the highest levels. As a business executive with a seat on high-profile corporate boards. And as a bestselling author and arbiter of manners. I was often the only woman in the room; this didn't change much as my achievements grew, as our education levels increased, and as the years passed. Even now, women aren't well represented in top positions. Thank goodness for *Break Your Own Rules*. This is the first book that lets us reimagine leadership—and I mean *really* reimagine leadership—by showing exactly how smart, skilled, and ambitious women can navigate the hurdles and reach their full potential. Don't wait to read this important book. You'll see leadership, and yourself, in a new and limitless way."

—Letitia Baldrige, business leader, philanthropist, former chief of staff for Jacqueline Kennedy, and proud octogenarian

"*Break Your Own Rules* reflects the experience of many women—nearly 2,000 Fortune 1000 executives and 5,000 professional women. But mostly, it addresses the pivotal question, 'What does it really take for women to lead today?' Authors Flynn, Heath, and Holt, having held executive positions themselves in addition to their time spent advising women and organizations on how to advance women's careers, provide some new and helpful insights and answers to this unfortunately persistent question. Get their help to move yourself forward faster. Their advice can make a difference."

—Crandall Close Bowles, chairman and CEO,
Springs Global (retired)

"Leadership is about winning and reaping big rewards. But getting to and staying at the top isn't easy. In fact, the hard truth is that for women, it remains highly improbable—unless you have a concrete strategy and learn how to lead in ways you can't imagine when you start. As one of the very few women who advises Fortune 500 CEOs and their teams every day, I know what it takes. So do *Break Your Own Rules* authors Flynn, Heath, and Holt. This is a hands-on guide that gets it right. Every woman who cares about her impact and leadership needs to get a copy of this game-changing book today."

—Saj-nicole Joni, confidential CEO advisor; bestselling author of *The Right Fight: How Great Leaders Use Healthy Conflict to Drive Performance, Innovation, and Value*

"I confess that I'm not sympathetic when I hear women say things like, 'I don't have a real shot at the top because relationships are formed on the golf course and I'm not a golfer.' Or, 'So-and-so is plotting and scheming for the position I want and I just won't play those games.' Or, 'People don't listen to me because I'm a woman.' I hear this last one from women a lot, and I think the reason nobody listens to them is because they say things like that! I'm not suggesting that barriers don't exist. The glass ceiling is still very real in many industries, and sadly, gender discrimination in the workplace still exists. But it's time for women to stop denying any accountability for the struggles they face, and instead, adopt the powerful, road-tested practices outlined in *Break Your Own Rules*, guaranteed to help women everywhere achieve their greatest potential. I love this book. It is fierce, a must-read!"

—Susan Scott, founder of the global training company Fierce Inc.; bestselling author of *Fierce Conversations: Achieving Success at Work & in Life—One Conversation at a Time* and *Fierce Leadership: A Bold Alternative to the Worst "Best" Practices of Business Today*

"Now is the time for women to claim their seats at the table. Whether in the board room or at the executive level, when women are represented, they consistently demonstrate their power to increase the bottom line and drive innovation. What I have seen in my work with women leaders around the world is that when passion, talent, and commitment are matched with a strategy to succeed, there's no limit in our ability to transform companies, communities, and even our world. That's exactly what you'll get from leadership experts Flynn, Heath, and Holt in *Break Your Own Rules*. The book delivers the very best of their experiences as executives and coaches, plus the latest research and untold stories from a number of women who have made it to the top and are making a significant impact. I urge you to pick up your copy today."

—Alyse Nelson, president/CEO, Vital Voices Global Partnership; social entrepreneur

"After four decades of women entering every segment of the American workforce, the percentage of women in senior leadership positions is barely a low double digit. When it comes to reaching the elite top ranks, solutions have been elusive—until now. In *Break Your Own Rules*, authors Flynn, Heath, and Holt build on their deep experience to offer real-life advice that really works. Women and men must read this compelling book. Now."

—Ruth Shaw, CEO and president of Duke Power (retired)

BREAK YOUR OWN RULES

How to Change the Patterns of Thinking That Block Women's Paths to Power

Jill Flynn | Kathryn Heath | Mary Davis Holt

Foreword by Sharon Allen

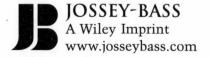

JOSSEY-BASS
A Wiley Imprint
www.josseybass.com

Published by Jossey-Bass
A Wiley Imprint
989 Market Street, San Francisco, CA 94103-1741—www.josseybass.com

Jossey-Bass books and products are available through most bookstores. To contact Jossey-Bass directly call our Customer Care Department within the U.S. at 800-956-7739, outside the U.S. at 317-572-3986, or fax 317-572-4002.

Wiley also publishes its books in a variety of electronic formats and by print-on-demand. Not all content that is available in standard print versions of this book may appear or be packaged in all book formats. If you have purchased a version of this book that did not include media that is referenced by or accompanies a standard print version, you may request this media by visiting http://booksupport.wiley.com. For more information about Wiley products, visit us www.wiley.com.

Library of Congress Cataloging-in-Publication Data

Flynn, Jill, 1945-
  Break your own rules : how to change the patterns of thinking that block women's paths to power / Jill Flynn, Kathryn Heath, Mary Davis Holt.—1st ed.
    p. cm.
  Includes bibliographical references and index.
  ISBN 978-1-118-06254-8 (hardback); ISBN 978-1-118-10381-4 (ebk);
ISBN 978-1-118-10382-1 (ebk); ISBN 978-1-118-10383-8 (ebk)
   1. Women executives—Psychology. 2. Businesswomen—Psychology. 3. Assertiveness in women. 4. Women—Promotions. 5. Success in business. I. Heath, Kathryn, 1949- II. Holt, Mary Davis, 1950- III. Title.
  HD6054.3.F584 2011
  658.4'09019—dc23

                                                                    2011021318

Printed in the United States of America
FIRST EDITION
HB Printing 10 9 8 7 6 5 4 3 2 1

To our amazing husbands,
Smitty, Tom, and David, who are our best friends
and our biggest fans

CONTENTS

FOREWORD

In business and in life, rules are everywhere.

Consider my own profession, in which there are well-documented rules to help accountants achieve consistency in everything from recognizing revenue to conducting an audit. Rules make financial reporting more uniform and enable investors to better compare the financial performance of various organizations.

But in life, and particularly in the business lives of women, there are ways of thinking that can begin to *feel like rules that must be consistently obeyed*. They encompass a wide range of behaviors, from being modest and playing it safe to focusing on others and seeking approval. Following such preconceived notions with blind obedience can inhibit, if not derail, a woman's ability to advance to senior leadership.

What makes traps like these so difficult for high-potential women to avoid, however, is that they are often *self-imposed*. Over time, patterns of thought driven by cultural norms or business tradition can harden into "rules" that often share a common thread—the misguided notion that a woman's work, talent, and ability to lead will stand out through her ability to blend in.

I know. One experience I had during an early assignment with Deloitte kept me from proceeding as quickly as I could to my next assignment. My "rule" was that it was inappropriate to let others—especially my superiors—know about my accomplishments. I thought that doing so was just like boasting and constituted unacceptable behavior. Furthermore, I reasoned that my boss had to be aware of all of my "good work." After all, he saw it every day—or so I thought. [You can read more on pages 73–74 of this book.]

This experience and others made me think—and, eventually, I realized that I needed to challenge in my own mind various rules that I had long accepted without question.

Ultimately, this process would lead me to break another rule of conventional business wisdom. When I became a Deloitte audit partner at my home office in Boise, Idaho, it was widely accepted that to "get ahead," you had to relocate to a larger office where you could display your talents on a bigger stage. But, for me, there was just one hitch. My husband, Rich, had his own business that was based in Boise. We were a classic two-career family—and moving just wasn't going to work for us. At least not then.

So I didn't move—for more than twenty years!

You might think that this would have kept me from taking on bold new challenges that could accelerate my growth as a leader.

But, in reality, I *had* grown immensely during my time in Boise—and on *my* terms. The time I spent there allowed me to learn every facet of our business inside and out, from recruiting to business development to managing the P&L, in addition to serving clients. During that time I also became involved in a number of national activities and initiatives. Such broad experience enabled me to perceive the bigger picture, which would prove invaluable as I moved forward to positions of increased responsibility and leadership.

When the time was right, I did move on. Rich had sold his business, and I eventually chose to accept a more substantial leadership role with Deloitte in Portland. Two years later, I chose to move again—this time to Los Angeles to become managing partner of what was then Deloitte's second-largest region. Although my path to senior leadership was unorthodox, it was absolutely the right path for me to take. And I did make it all the way to chairman! What I discovered along the way was another self-imposed rule, but this one I will always follow: if I am to lead others effectively, I must first practice the self-leadership of being true to myself.

Break Your Own Rules is a book about women being true to themselves at every stage of their journey—by understanding the thinking that can entangle us in webs of our own making. This book identifies the self-defeating patterns of thought that burden so many women today, and articulates new approaches that can help women break free to pursue the exciting opportunities of tomorrow.

The research conducted by its authors reveals thought-provoking findings born from years of experience. Before establishing the successful leadership consulting firm that bears their names, Jill Flynn, Kathryn Heath, and Mary Davis Holt navigated their own paths to the C suites and board rooms of leading corporations—and once they arrived there, they excelled. For many years, Deloitte has asked Flynn Heath Holt Leadership to share with our aspiring women leaders what its founders have learned from their experiences. The feedback from that training—as well as the results—have been impressive.

I am confident that the thinking to be found in the pages that follow will enable many more women to take their rightful place as senior leaders. Like glass ceilings, Old Rules that limit women were made to be broken.

This book will show you how—with thoughtfulness, insight, and resolve.

May 2011   Sharon Allen
                                             Chairman of the Board
                                                      Deloitte LLP

BREAK YOUR OWN RULES

1

OUR VISION

We have a dream. It is a big vision ... it is a leap ... and it is audacious: we want to see women make up at least 30 percent of the top leadership positions in corporate America within the next ten years. We believe that 30 percent will be a tipping point. When 30 percent of corporate leaders are women, the goals and direction of corporate America will change. The Old Rules will be shattered. America's corporations will be better led, and everyone will benefit.

This is the vision we're pushing toward each and every day. This book is the culmination of what we've learned over the last decade spent coaching thousands of women executives. It debunks the faulty assumptions that limit many of you as women, and it introduces a new set of rules to help you adopt thoughts and actions that are conducive to power. Using research we've conducted over a multiyear period and the patterns we've identified through coaching high-potential women, we'll tell you how to improve your odds of success at the highest levels of leadership by thinking differently and breaking your own rules.

We have a way to go before our vision becomes a reality. Despite the positive impact women leaders have on corporate performance,[1] very few of us hold the top slots in major organizations. As of now, there are just thirteen women CEOs steering Fortune 500 companies.[2] That translates to less than a lowly 3 percent—and the number hasn't risen in recent years. For each new woman who enters Fortune's list, another falls off. This is a kick in the gut, considering that women not only outnumber men as a percentage of the total workforce but also earn more undergraduate and graduate degrees than men.[3]

And then there is the matter of take-home pay. According to the Bureau of Labor Statistics, women's wages came in at about 79 percent of men's in 2008. We won't dispute that there has been some progress made in recent decades, but the wage gap still exists, and it's significant.[4]

In an age when more women are taking over power positions in global politics, poor representation in the business sector and the lack of equity are surprising. Something's very wrong here. Some of this is certainly gender bias; that much we know. If you believe that human nature dictates that senior leaders hire people who are like themselves, then you will figure that men open the gate for other men, and women don't rise through the ranks as easily. We also have stereotypes to contend with, which cast doubts on women's leadership style and even our competitive drive.

These interrelated realities persist despite the fact that they are proven to be bad for business. Research published by Deloitte, for example, argues that companies with women leaders perform better.[5] The report points to a higher return on equity and higher return on sales for companies with more women board directors.[6] Another study that tracked fifteen hundred U.S. companies from 1992 to 2006 found a direct positive correlation between the number of senior women managers and financial performance, including market value of the firm, sales growth, and return on equity.[7] After all, what better way to be sure that your products and services reflect the true needs of female consumers and decision makers— with all that purchasing power—than by having adequate female representation at the top of your corporation?

One study out of Pepperdine University, conducted over a nineteen-year period, determined that those firms with a higher number of women executives outperformed their competitors on key financial measures, including profitability and return on assets.[8] Sylvia Ann Hewlett, founder and president of the Center for Work-Life Policy, corroborates these findings: "The fewer female managers a company has, the greater drop in its share price since January 2008. The facts couldn't be clearer: smart women equal stronger companies."[9]

Studies also indicate that having women in the boardroom improves corporate governance. According to The Conference Board of Canada, boards with more women tend to pay greater attention to audit and risk oversight, and they take into account the needs of more categories of stakeholders.[10]

Despite the proven benefits women leaders bring to organizations, the challenges we face remain numerous and complex. In a landmark 2007 study, Catalyst found that because women are held to a masculine standard of leadership, we are left with unfavorable options no matter how we perform as leaders. This double bind can undermine our opportunities. In other words, when we are perceived as failing to exhibit certain traditionally male leadership traits, we are considered to be incompetent; but when we do exhibit those traits, we are looked upon as unfeminine.[11]

It's time we nipped all of this in the bud. There are other avenues to consider—ones that are actually within our control and can make a difference right now.

What We Believe

Behavioral psychology tells us that the way humans think and the corresponding decisions they make are not always in their own best self-interest. In our coaching engagements, we use what we've learned about how successful women executives think—and we help our female clients put that thinking to work to level the playing field for all of us.

Technical knowledge in one's field is essential, and leadership skills are crucial. However, we have found that for women who are at midcareer or near the top, building career momentum is not a matter of adding skills. It is about determining what's keeping you where you are and figuring out how you might be getting in your own way.

We believe that for women to rise to the highest ranks in business, we need to unwind some of our traditional thinking and break our own rules. We have to rethink the conversations we are having in our heads and tell ourselves a new story. We will review many of these old thinking patterns throughout this book—getting to their root cause and suggesting new ways of thinking that will work better. You can bet that Andrea Jung, CEO of Avon, and Indra Nooyi, CEO of PepsiCo, are not using outdated mental models and thinking themselves out of power.

We all have thoughts and beliefs that limit our potential. Some of these beliefs come from our individual experiences; they take hold over the years. *I'm not good at taking credit. I'm much better working behind the scenes. I'm lucky to have this job—any job.* Others are a result of the gender stereotypes that are all around us. They creep into our heads over time. *It's my job to nurture everyone else before I take care of my own needs. I am selfish and self-centered if I choose to "indulge" my ambition.* Still others are simply erroneous conventional wisdom. *I can have it all without compromise. I'm a failure if I can't make it look easy. That's a job for someone else—not for me.*

We get in our own way when we buy into limiting beliefs. But we don't have to continue repeating the same patterns. We have it within our power to change our own thinking and therefore change our future. We can nurture the beliefs that will sustain us and help us grow. As women, we have been taught as children, in school, and on the job to behave in certain ways. In contrast, our research and years of experience coaching women executives on the rise tell us that what we really need to do to succeed at the highest levels in business is to *think differently*. The New Rules in this book will help you do just that.

Research and Experience

When the three of us began our corporate careers in the 1980s, we believed that it was a matter of ten years before women would gain parity with men at all levels. It turns out that were we naive—very naive. Over the years, we did exactly what you are doing. We worked hard, became self-confident, achieved notable success, and gained the respect of our colleagues. Yes, we each experienced setbacks. We wondered many times what was really going on and why the world of business was hard to decipher, often disappointing, and sometimes downright unfair. But, like you, we pushed ahead. We managed hundreds of people, oversaw multimillion-dollar budgets, and executed mergers and reorganizations. On the way to the executive suite, we figured out some things that helped us become successful senior leaders. After twenty-year careers, each of us left our corporate job and began our second act. We decided to use what we learned to help other women succeed.

Over the past decade, we've coached and trained over five thousand professional women across America, mostly mid- and upper-level managers in large, hierarchical companies. As a part of that process, we use surveys and interviews to assess our clients' current level of leadership effectiveness and pinpoint high-leverage areas where behavior change will have a positive impact.

The specific findings on which this book is based and the corresponding advice we deliver were born not just from years of firsthand business experience but also from our research conducted over a decade. Our consulting approach is evidence based. In the course of our work, we've interviewed more than seventeen hundred executives to find out how they thought women could be more successful and get promoted. We use a standard set of interview questions, and we code concepts and common answers in order to uncover the consistencies and trends; these form the basis of our approach and the guidance in this book. Furthermore, we've surveyed thirty-five hundred people, including the managers, subordinates, and colleagues who work with each of the women we coach. We use what they tell us about how a woman is effective or ineffective to assess how an individual woman's understanding of her own behavior matches what other people perceive to be true about her.

The themes in this book are a summary of what all our interviews, surveys, and coaching sessions have taught us. There were a few surprises and a lot of themes we would have predicted. Overall, there were several strong threads that led us to our conclusions.

Throughout this book, you'll read stories about the women we coach, but you'll also hear our own stories and what we've learned through our firsthand business experience. In addition, we've interviewed eight well-known female executives—current and former CEOs and senior leaders—who graciously offered unvarnished insights and stories. These interviews have been conducted specifically for this book.

We are passionate about equipping women leaders for success. The ideas in this book have resonated with the women we coach, and we've been able to see firsthand the impact they have had on the confidence and overall success of our longtime clients. Our research has caused us to have a distinctive point of view about how people change, and the foundation of our perspective is that success is dictated by the thinking that drives our actions.

Our Red-Suit Vision

In our leadership development programs, we encourage women to be very clear about their personal career visions and to become visionary, inspirational leaders for their own corporations. We're going to practice what we preach and share more about the big vision we have for Flynn Heath Holt Leadership.

We mentioned our dream: women in at least 30 percent of the top leadership positions in corporate America. Now we want to paint a picture for you of what that would look like, because we believe that a picture will inspire you as it has us.

Picture a boardroom. There are typically eight to twelve people on a board these days, so let's assume there are ten at this table. We know that today 17 percent of all corporate board members are women. Imagine there is one woman at this table—you. You are wearing a red suit. The other nine people at the table are men, and they are wearing their gray suits.

When we change the number to 30 percent women at the top, there will be three red suits at that table. Imagine how differently you would feel if you had two other red suits at the table with you. We can assure you, having sat at that corporate board table ourselves, that it is very different when you are the only red suit as opposed to when there are other women whose voices are heard along with your own.

Now let's look at Fortune 500 CEOs. There are thirteen female CEOs serving right now, so there are thirteen red suits out of five hundred. Imagine a ballroom with five hundred people sitting in fifty rows of ten people each. The front row is all red suits, and there are three women in the second row; the rest are all gray suits. Now imagine that 30 percent of the CEOs are women. There will be fifteen rows of women in red suits, and the other thirty-five rows will be all men in gray suits. Now the room is very different.

Finally, go with us to an arena where we have taken all of the top corporate leaders in America. Right now, one end would be in red. Women on one end, that's it. The rest—both sides and the other end—are men in gray. When we get to our 30 percent goal, *one whole side* will be red suits, and the rest will be gray. We hope you can envision what we are talking about and what a big change this would be. Not only will the business environment for women be altered dramatically, but the entire discussion at the top of corporate America would change completely.

Now imagine that your red suit gives you the confidence and courage to become a powerful executive. This book will help you put on that suit every day and go out there to pursue your own *big vision*. Maybe it is to be CEO of your corporation. Maybe it is to run a division of your company. Maybe it is to serve on a corporate board. Whatever your big vision is, we want to help you get there. We want to help you break your own rules—the ones that are holding you back. This book will give you insight into your own thinking and behavior. It will help you begin to make your personal career vision come true. If you do that, you'll make our big vision real as well.

This Book

We'll start in Chapter Two by examining the Old Rules that hold us back. We'll introduce and describe each Old Rule, explore a little about where it comes from, and mention why it is problematic for women.

Chapters Three through Eight go into greater detail and contain a few consistent elements:

Stories. We work with real women every day who, like you, are building their careers and breaking through barriers in their professional and personal lives. The most successful clients we've worked with, including many who have gone on to lead business units and divisions, have experienced challenges and setbacks along the way. We've presented true accounts, some of which are composites, to demonstrate the common issues so many of us face and how to move past these obstacles to become much stronger and more focused on success. We will also include stories and advice from some of the most successful and savvy women running businesses today.

The Old Rules. The first part of each chapter will tackle one of the old-school notions that our research and experience have identified as a rule that should be broken. We'll identify the origin and impact of each Old Rule, also exploring several related subsets, and lay the groundwork for better thinking and a mind-set that is focused on advancement.

The New Rules. The second part of each chapter presents a New Rule. Our emphasis here is on actionable and practical advice that will make it easier for you to envision putting the New Rule into practice. This is the guidance that we use every day in our coaching sessions. As always, we've kept it real—with practical and specific tips you can use immediately.

The final chapter brings all of our advice together and presents a general call to action. We challenge you to close ranks and work together to continue to carve out your own careers and to identify opportunities that are attractive and accessible to women. We believe that to achieve our goal of 30 percent at the top, women must come together in solidarity to propel each other forward.

So put on your red suit and start your journey by examining the Old Rules that are holding you back from success.

2

BREAK YOUR OWN RULES

I think I've figured out this career thing. In order to move up to a more senior position, I'll have to break some of my own rules.

—KAY, COACHING CLIENT

Even though we don't know you personally, we know a lot about you. You are smart, well educated, articulate, hardworking, competitive, driven, and full of energy. You have been building your career for at least a dozen years. You like where you are. You have confidence in your professional expertise, you've achieved outstanding results, you've been promoted several times, and you have the respect of your peers and superiors. What's more, you are probably earning even more than you thought you would when you started your career.

At the same time, you are not exactly where you want to be in your career, and getting to that elusive next level is proving to be difficult. You work long hours, but you can't seem to gain enough traction. You overcommit at work and at home and are constantly reworking your calendar; you have a sneaking feeling that you are not making as much money as most of your male peers.

Despite all of this, you remain optimistic that you will succeed. And we know that you're right. You are very much like the women we coach: engaged, on the rise, yet still looking for an edge to help you leap over the latest rock-hard career hurdle. Many of the women we work with tell us that they feel at a greater disadvantage the higher they rise in their organizations. These are some of the phrases we've heard time and again:

"For some reason my voice isn't being heard."
"I'm not offered the types of opportunities I really want—and I
   don't know why."
"I'm feeling stuck, but I don't know what I want to do next."
"I'm not advancing, but I don't have any more to give."

In our coaching sessions with women who want to break into top leadership roles, we propose simple steps to help them increase their chances of success. These steps require women to make adjustments in how they think about themselves. We'll offer you the same advice in this book:

By thinking differently, you'll find it much easier to act differently. By acting differently, your voice will heard, and you will be considered for the job opportunities you really want.

One woman whom Jill was coaching, a crackerjack financial professional named Kay, hit the nail right on the head. After listening to Kay talk about her career aspirations, Jill observed that Kay very clearly wanted bigger opportunities and a broader leadership role. She wanted to see some progress in her career—yet she was doing the exact same things she'd always done and in the exact same ways. They were easy, they were natural—but they weren't working.

Jill helped Kay see why the things that had gotten her noticed and promoted in the past weren't going to do it for her as she climbed into a senior leadership role. She would need to make some fundamental changes. Kay replied, "I think I've figured out this career thing. In order to move up to a more senior position, I'll have to break some of my own rules." She was exactly right.

To move into an executive role, you'll have to break some of your own rules; these are the beliefs and attitudes about yourself and the workplace that have gotten you this far. As Marshall Goldsmith has said, "What got you here won't get you there."[1] It's one thing to get your foot in the door and begin to prove yourself at a company. You deal with tough clients, you hire the right people and develop your team, and you bring in business. All of this sets you up for success. However, it's another thing entirely to begin to scale the heights of an organization and to put yourself in line for the top jobs. The mind-set at the top is completely different.

In this book, we present the new thinking that we believe will get you there. We call this thinking the New Rules—and we will explore it in detail in the chapters that follow. Our in-depth research and the lessons each of us has learned from making many mistakes of our own have shown us that these New Rules are decisive in propelling women into the next phases of their careers. We know that you have already mastered some of these rules, or you wouldn't be where you are today. Going even further in business, however, means opening yourself up to different ways of thinking and acting.

The Old Rules

Before we proceed, let's have a look at the Old Rules. Keep in mind that we are not labeling these thoughts and behaviors as "bad." The fact is, we've *been there* and have made all of these mistakes ourselves along the way. We identify with you and with the women we coach every day. Our hope is that by reading this book you'll be able to bypass some of these stumbling blocks on your way to career success.

Focus on Others (Instead of Taking Center Stage)

We've discovered that many talented women find it natural to focus their attention on helping others succeed instead of spending their precious time nurturing their own career success. They feel selfish and self-centered saying no when people all around them ask for help or assistance, and they oftentimes fail to take credit for their own accomplishments. We will coach you to take your own career dreams and aspirations seriously. This is the first fundamental step to breaking your own rules.

Seek Approval (Instead of Proceeding Until Apprehended)

In our coaching sessions, we've worked with countless women executives who are exceptionally collaborative leaders. They like to be liked, but the desire for consensus and buy-in can sometimes slow them down. We've made it our mission to help women retain their core strengths while at the same time acting decisively to make things happen. We'll tell you how to change your thinking in order to proceed on your own authority and do so effectively and with confidence.

Be Modest (Instead of Projecting Personal Power)

Many women who are motivated to move into leadership positions are nonetheless ambivalent about projecting power. Modesty and self-deprecation come more naturally. We've seen women come off as downright apologetic in the face of success—as if it does not suit them or they don't deserve it. We'll unwind the self-limiting beliefs that cause women to distance themselves from projecting personal power at work. Then we will tell you how to adjust your thinking and dial up your comfort level in order to feel at home in a position of power and authority.

Work Harder (Instead of Being Politically Savvy)

Many women are disappointed when their hard work and long hours don't seem to pay off in terms of career advancement. But working harder is not the key to getting promoted, and it's certainly not going to deliver the life you want. We will demonstrate how to build your career as if you were running for office—creating a platform, lining up sponsors, putting together a coalition—and then do it over and over again as your career goals change.

Play It Safe (Instead of Playing to Win)

If you want to set yourself apart, you have to play to win. This includes making yourself visible and taking the lead in high-stakes situations. Selling and negotiation skills are one part of the equation. Putting yourself out there also means becoming comfortable with risk and the possibility of failure. Many of the women we work with seem to lack confidence in their ability to deliver—even after they've proven themselves countless times. We'll demonstrate how to stop letting others take the lead and to think differently in order to become more comfortable living with risk.

It's All or Nothing (Instead of Both-And)

Black-and-white thinking does not lead to career success or personal satisfaction. Because complexity and constant change are everywhere in business and in our world today, dealing with ambiguity has become a primary leadership trait that women need to master. One phrase that has crept into dozens of our coaching files over the years is the notion of *having it all*. It's no coincidence that many of the women who are trying to have it all are also the ones who are most disappointed and frustrated. This is just one example of the type of extreme thinking that pushes us off the path to success.

Changing How You Think About Change

In our work, we've found that having certain conditions in place make it much more likely for women to achieve notable success in their careers. These conditions include

- *Women-friendly workplace policies and practices*. Not all orga-nizations are committed to practices and policies that support women. Clearly, it's better if you can work for an organization that is.
- *Personal support*. Does your family and your personal network support you in your quest for career success?
- *Key skills and behaviors*. You must not only demonstrate exper-tise in your functional area but also cultivate executive skills.
- *Plum assignments and challenges*. You need to step up for the jobs that will give you experience and get you noticed.
- *Active sponsorship*. Do you have a group of three or four executive supporters who can the open doors that will lead to career advancement?

All of these conditions are critical for you as a woman to succeed in your career. However, we've found that above and beyond these conditions, the single most critical factor in success is how women think. Because our thinking directly influences our behavior, it can be either an advantage or a handicap.

There are a few reasons for our focus on women's thinking. First, this is the area we key into most frequently when we coach women. When we first started out as executive coaches, we assumed that if we helped women improve their skills, that would be enough. Not so: the thinking that motivates behavior is the fuel that sustains the behavior. Second, although all the conditions we listed are important for advancement, some are within your control and some are not. Our goal in this book is to focus on the areas you know you can change and control.

Years ago, a friend of ours was going through a divorce, and she was feeling understandably unhappy and confused. She wondered why her marriage didn't work out despite her good efforts and intentions. She turned to her sister for some tea and sympathy, expecting a soft shoulder and comforting words. Her sister offered advice that surprised her. She said, "You need to figure out what your role in the break-up was. Why not take responsibility for your 50 percent of the situation?" It turned out to be great advice. Our friend transformed a difficult and painful situation into an opportunity to explore and improve herself. When she later remarried, the hard work she did to address "her 50 percent" was one big factor in building a successful relationship.

Why wait for a crisis (in your relationship or your career) to focus on the factors that you can improve and control?

Changing your ways is not easy. The fact that change is inevitable in today's world doesn't seem to make it any easier. We all have emotional triggers to contend with as well as a lifetime of experience that guides our thinking and behavior. The three of us each have our own way of coaching women to get through their change process. Kathryn, for example, likes to ask her clients to alter their *perception* of change. As a collector of prints and paintings, she will occasionally buy one at an estate sale or gallery. Before it hangs in her home, she will have it reframed to suit the décor of a certain room. The piece itself stays the same no matter what the frame looks like—the colors, texture, and shape of the painting don't change. But it's amazing how much the new framing can alter the overall look of the piece. It's the same picture, but it somehow looks so much better! The same concept holds true in a lot of situations where personal change is required.

We're not asking you to change who you are, compromise your values, or violate your integrity. You do not need to leave your old ways behind completely. What we're advocating is that you reframe how you think about yourself—what stories you tell yourself and how you see the career opportunities that lie ahead of you. There's no magic bullet. Changing your thinking simply requires some time and effort—but you'll see career benefits before long.

We realize that the path to power is not easy for women. We struggle with the double binds: if we act in ways perceived to be feminine, then we are seen as ineffective; if we do not, then we are seen as unlikable. It's difficult to figure out how to get it right. Have you ever hiked the path down into the center of the Grand Canyon? It's a narrow path filled with rocks and twists. It's treacherously steep, and there's no railing. From our experience, that's a lot like a woman's path to power. It's filled with emotional challenges as well as logistical and practical obstacles. It's a long, winding, and narrow path, but plenty of women have walked it successfully, and you can too.

3

TAKE CENTER STAGE

All the world's a stage.
—WILLIAM SHAKESPEARE

FOCUS ON OTHERS ⟶ TAKE CENTER STAGE

Jess was one of those women who told us that she strived to be Superwoman. And most people who knew her felt that she was pretty close: she had a prestigious and well-paying job. Attractive, with big brown eyes, she always had a smile on her face. She traveled to see a West Coast client once a month from her home in suburban Connecticut, and she had business meetings in Singapore twice a year. The seats in her Honda Pilot were filled with clean, adorable children, ages three through eleven—including two she and her husband adopted from overseas. Jess was a two-time marathoner, always on the prowl for her next race or a quick triathlon. She also made it to a few school field trips each semester. Everything seemed perfect. But was it?

During our coaching process with Jess, her seemingly perfect life started to come apart at the seams. The trouble began with a few sporadic migraines. At first, even the slowly creeping fatigue couldn't keep her from her 5 A.M. run. Finally, however, the exhaustion won out. Jess missed an important client meeting as well as her boss's leadership team meeting. A couple of days after that, she landed in the hospital. The doctor said it was severe fatigue that could and would lead to something more serious if she didn't take a break. He said she needed a rest, and for once she didn't disagree.

Jess told us afterward that she felt responsible for everyone in her life—her family, her clients, her team at work. She believed she was the only one who could keep all the balls in the air. If she didn't do it, it wouldn't get done.

No two women are the same, and Jess's experience is admittedly extreme. Still, we coach women every day who are driving themselves to the edge of sanity because they believe they need to focus on everyone except themselves. *My clients can't do without me. My kids (husband, mother, team, fill in the blank) really need me. I'm the only one who knows how to do this. My boss is counting on me to finish this.* And so on.

In our work, we've found that many of the smartest women around the table focus their attention on what other people need, and they leave no time or energy to help *themselves* thrive professionally and personally.

What Were We Thinking?

Unsurprisingly, most of our female clients say they feel emotionally drawn to care for and support the people around them. Empathy is a human emotion that many scientists believe is built into our chemistry. According to research from the University of California, Berkeley, genetic factors cause women, in general, to be more empathic than men.[1] The hormone oxytocin, for example, best known for its role as a catalyst for inducing labor, is believed to increase our desire to bond with others. Higher levels of this chemical in women enable us to nurture and respond to the emotional needs of our offspring and others around us. Biology, including brain structure, makes women and men react differently in everyday situations as well as in the high-stress moments we all experience at work. For example, research indicates that women are perceived to be more emotionally intelligent than men.[2] But as Jess learned, the tendency to put others first can cause us to be less strategic and more prone to self-sacrifice.

And it's also bad for our health. According to Elizabeth Shirt-cliff, a psychologist and behavioral endocrinologist at the University of New Orleans, our natural inclination to empathize could be making us sick. Feeling someone else's pain, she told MSNBC, "comes at a cost, and that cost is the higher preponderance of anxiety and depressive disorders in women."[3]

But there's more to this dilemma than hormones and neurotransmitters. The searing guilt many of us feel when we devote time to our careers and are away from our families—or when we leave the office early to go to our child's ballet recital—is also a product of our upbringing and environment.

Our sense of self begins to develop when we are children, as we receive messages from a multitude of people and from the media and beyond. Caregivers, as well as peers and teachers, are our primary influences on gender identity.[4] We internalize the role models we see and the expectations assigned to us at an early age and carry them with us as we become adults, have families of our own, and build our careers.[5]

The bottom line is that our individual behavior is a consequence of social and cultural expectations, in addition to our individual dispositions. All of this baggage and history leaves a mark. The desire to succeed and to please our parents—or perhaps to be different from our parents—not to mention all of our other X chromosome tendencies, can result in some ineffective patterns of thinking and behaviors that don't work for us in the workplace.

Our drive to nurture those around us and still live up to our own unrealistic expectations for success can be exhausting.

Our Research

We would not have predicted that the need to take center stage would emerge as a rule, but in our interviews about what women need to do in order to be successful at senior levels, it came up frequently. In our interviews with high-level business executives, we heard comments like these:

"She needs to quit being backstage and get on stage."

"She needs to ask for help. She gets loaded up with the work she does for everyone else and flames out. It is dangerous for her and for our company. It is risky."

"She is a mother hen. I think this is a strength, but she has to also learn to say no and guard her time."

"She needs to focus on herself and get herself in the limelight."

The women we coach say to us:

"I am afraid that if I delegate, they will think I am not doing my job."

"When I start the day, I always say that I am going to make some time for myself. What I find is that it is 6 P.M., and I've solved everyone else's problems and did not solve mine . . . and I am exhausted."

"I prefer to be behind the scenes."

"I really want a big job, but I am afraid that if I put it out there, no one will think I deserve it."

The Old Rule: Focus on Others

In our work, we have found that there are specific beliefs and thoughts women have that are associated with this Old Rule thinking. Here are some of the most common:

THE OLD RULES

1. I must take care of everyone else.
2. My needs come last.
3. It's not okay to ask for help.
4. I'm a great number two.
5. I don't belong on center stage.

I Must Take Care of Everyone Else

One thing we heard from Jess after her stint in the hospital was that she felt personally responsible for a long list of people. She mentored her employees and took their professional development very seriously. Her clients loved her because she gave them her cell phone number and made herself available to problem-solve at all hours of the day and night. She helped out at her kids' schools when the teacher asked for volunteers. And on. And on. As women, and as people, of course we want to help our employees and colleagues succeed. Of course we want to do everything possible to show our families that we love and support them. But we need to take our own dreams and goals seriously as well.

As Jess found out, taking responsibility for everyone else can lead to burnout. When we see women feeling overwhelmed and denying their exhaustion and frustration, we say, "She's French fried." That's our phrase to describe the overwhelming fatigue that eventually comes when you nurture everyone around you and are surprised when the cracks start to appear. But they will appear . . . and continue to spread unless you make some choices.

My Needs Come Last

This is the flip side of the "caring for others" coin. If you focus all of your time and energy on fulfilling the needs of colleagues and clients, not to mention your family members, when exactly can you attend to your own needs? Dead last.

A woman we coach, Denise, took this Old Rule to new heights. As a midlevel manager in a financial services firm, she was considered by colleagues to be a fast riser. She had great technical skills and was also naturally adept at handling relationships. Managing difficult personalities was her specialty. For years she demonstrated an aptitude for leadership and the ability to come through in a pinch. So when a senior-level position in her company opened up, Denise was the first person her boss recommended. It meant greater responsibility and more money. These were things that Denise had said she wanted for herself. It seemed so win-win. But everyone was taken by surprise when she declined the offer. She said the timing was not right for her.

The timing wasn't right? Her boss was astounded. When we sat down to talk with Denise about her decision, she said that if she accepted a promotion now, she couldn't live up to her current obligations. She was right in the middle of a complex, detail-heavy client project that she couldn't just dump on someone else. She had just hired a new associate and felt obligated to show him the ropes. Her twin teens were taking their PSATs and needed her help and support. And so on and so on. But what about Denise? This promotion was something she'd wanted for years, but she decided to turn it down because she felt guilty putting her needs and desires first. We wanted to say, "What were you thinking?" but we know what she was thinking, and she's not the only one.

She was thinking that her own career needs, interests, and ambitions were unimportant. She was blind to the fact that she might never get a second chance at this type of career advancement. She put herself last on the list—again. Do you do the same thing? If so, you need to examine why your dreams are taking a backseat. If you're allowing Old Rule thinking to sabotage your chances for career success, then it's time to replace it with New Rules that will work better for you.

It's Not Okay to Ask for Help

In the same way that some women feel obligated to help everyone around them succeed, many women are spending too much energy sweating the small stuff. Being a detail person can be great—as long as you are not holding on so tight that you fail to delegate and allow other people to help you.

We've heard hundreds of reasons why the women we coach don't like to ask for help, and we smile every time we hear a new excuse. These are a few of our favorites:

"My team lacks the experience to do this."
"If I have to show someone else how to do it, it will take me longer in the end."
"Too much is riding on this."
"I need to keep my eye on this one."

And the number-one reason we hear for a failure to delegate: "I'm the only one who can do this."

It's time to lighten up! No one is indispensable. Freeing yourself up to handle strategic tasks is a good thing for everyone. If you continue to hoard the detail work, you will inadvertently protect your status as a workhorse. We've all been there. You're faced with an important but mundane task that can and should be handed down, but you can't help but think *No one can do this quite as well as I can.*

One of our clients, Nancy, repeatedly found herself in this situation. When we told her it looked to us as if this was becoming a self-defeating pattern, she said, "This is different. I'm the only one who can do this work at the level the client requires." Okay, fair enough if that's really true. So we asked Nancy to answer one last question: "Would your male peers ever think of doing this job themselves?" Her answer was no. Nancy finally admitted that she was not working smart. She was trying to be perfect and make an A on everything, even B- and C-level tasks.

This particular Old Rule is tricky, and you will need some dedicated effort, commitment, and confidence to break it. Trust us—you won't regret making this change ... and the rest of your team will thank you.

I'm a Great Number Two

We hate this Old Rule because it holds so many great women back.

As the comedian Jim Carrey once said, "Behind every great man is a woman rolling her eyes." If you are a woman who excels in the number-two slot, you should ask yourself, *What am I doing?* Don't use success in a supporting role as an excuse to settle for less than the best.

Gloria was an excellent number two. She worked in the employee benefits area for a large multinational corporation. She was extremely advanced technically and was valued for her good judgment. Gloria was running the unit when it was combined with another group, and her counterpart, Lee, was promoted above her. "I like Lee very much, and I enjoy working for him. In fact, I'm his right arm. He counts on me," she said. "I'm flattered that he thinks so highly of me," she went on. "I'm really a good number two."

Even though she liked working for Lee, Gloria felt stuck. She believed that she needed Lee's permission to pursue projects that would allow her to advance. She felt a certain pride about doing her job so well that she was indispensible as someone's backup. But this was a trap for Gloria, and it can be a trap for you. There's no crime in deriving pleasure at being needed. Still, there's no need to settle for second-tier status. You are so damn close.

I Don't Belong on Center Stage

If this Old Rule resonates with you, you are not the only one. Many of the smart, successful women we know hate to be the focus of attention. They would rather remain safely behind the scenes. They defer, yield their time, fold their arms, smile lightly, and shrink to take up less space.

The fact is that some of us feel uncomfortable about having ambition. Our coaching files are full of conversations we've had with female clients who are struggling with the internal conflict between being ambitious and believing that others must not know that they are ambitious. Or perhaps it is because they don't feel worthy of success?

Cathy Bessant is a woman who has made it to the top echelon of corporate America. She is the global technology and operations executive at Bank of America and a member of the CEO's senior leadership team. By anybody's standard, Cathy would be considered

a "success"; however, she told us about a blinding glimpse of the
obvious that she recently had.

> I was talking to two colleagues recently about a new civic role
> I was being asked to take on as board chair of a large com-
> munity foundation. I said to them, "Well, I'm not sure I'm
> worthy, and I don't want to do anything to hurt the founda-
> tion. I want to make sure we keep the foundation at the center
> of things." That's actually what I said in response to being
> asked to take on this cool leadership position! And one of them
> just looked at me and said, "Would you stop playing that tape?
> A man would never say what you just said." She was right. Like
> many women of my generation, I was promoted quickly. All of
> a sudden you are in a bigger job without the proof point that
> gives you that important internal metric that says: I completely
> belong, I own this, this is me.

It's been our experience that women are as ambitious as men,
but many of us feel less entitled to lead than men do. In fact,
many women we work with spend an inordinate amount of time
preparing their colleagues to lead and succeed. Maybe that means
spending their evenings updating someone else's presentation or
prepping a colleague to meet with a key client. Whether this self-
limiting mentality is a result of nature or nurture is beside the point.
If there's a little voice in your head saying *I'm not worthy,* it's time
to break this miserable Old Rule once and for all.

Your Turn . . .

Before we move on to explore the New Rules, please take a moment
to answer a few questions. For you to change your thinking and
behavior, you need to have a baseline awareness of your personal

and professional goals. The questions posed in each chapter are intended to help you gain that awareness.

What are your biggest, wildest dreams for success in your career?

How do you "get in the way" of your career success by taking care of other people?

As a woman, is it okay for you to be ambitious? Why? Why not?

Are you comfortable being on center stage? Under what circumstances?

What is the story you tell yourself about why you don't take center stage?

Bonnie St. John is a special friend and colleague of ours. She is also an amazing and accomplished professional. Bonnie is perhaps most renowned as an international ski racing champion. Despite having her right leg amputated at age five, she won a silver and two bronze medals in the 1984 Paralympics in Innsbruck, Austria, thereby becoming the first African American ever to win Olympic medals in skiing. After the Paralympics, Bonnie went on to graduate with honors from Harvard, win a Rhodes Scholarship, and earn her master's degree in economics at Oxford. Bonnie has been featured on CNN and *Good Morning America*, in the *New York Times* and *O* magazine, and in many other national and international media outlets. When we were talking to Bonnie about how she got comfortable taking center stage, she told us an interesting story.

> You know, it is a funny thing, people write books and give speeches saying, "Do what you love and the money will come." I don't agree with that. I know a lot of people who are doing what they love, and they are practically broke. What I say is, "Do what you love and follow the money." Figure out what

makes sense economically. How can I do something that I love in a way that will pay me well? How can I have more success *and* more personal satisfaction in my life?

Satisfaction is subjective; it is very personal. I think you can have high satisfaction and high achievement, but many of us settle for high satisfaction and low achievement or high achievement and low satisfaction. I think we can all look for creative ways to find the high satisfaction, high achievement solution. In my case, when my daughter was young . . . I wanted more flexibility in my life. So I asked myself, how can I have a career where I can spend more time with my child?

Someone suggested to me that I would be a good keynote speaker—meaning that I should aim for the most elite opportunities with the biggest audiences. At first I could not imagine it! However, I let myself get used to the idea, and finally I was willing to own it for myself. I took my own dream seriously. I prepared to be a keynote speaker. I learned how to market myself as a keynote speaker, and I positioned myself as a keynote speaker, not as a trainer or a workshop presenter. And guess what? I gradually became a successful keynote speaker. It took time, but I did it. I think this is important advice for women in corporate America. You need to package yourself to be a center-stage person and think about building your career that way. You don't just fall into being a top speaker or a top corporate executive. You have to be very intentional about it.

Women need to understand that taking center stage doesn't mean that it is all about you. Yes, we as women like to focus on others, but if you are willing to take center stage, you can focus on other people in a much more powerful way. You can help people a lot more and support people a lot more, and you will be in a position to create conditions for other people's development. Look at it this way: by *not* taking center stage you are really being selfish.

The New Rule: Take Center Stage

As Bonnie St. John illustrates, having a firm vision of your own aspirations and strengths—and allowing other people to help you succeed—is good for you and everyone else around you. Achieving both success and satisfaction requires making choices that allow you to invest in yourself and live into the larger plan you have for yourself and your life. Let's look at the components of this New Rule and see how they've played out for some other women we know.

THE NEW RULES

1. Take your goals and dreams seriously.
2. Think bigger. Aim higher.
3. Just say no.
4. Be ruthless with your calendar.
5. Take time to refuel.
6. Get famous for something.
7. Practice taking center stage.

Take Your Goals and Dreams Seriously

Focusing on your personal goals instead of being the one who nurtures everyone around you requires a certain amount of courage.

A client of ours, Patty, found that courage. A tax accountant in a large global corporation, she had joined the company recently after thriving at a smaller organization. Known for her warm personality and quick wit, she was liked by everyone. She did a great job and was beginning to build a name for herself when we first met her. According to Patty, she left her previous employer in order to work at a place that could offer some new opportunities and upward mobility in the future.

After about a year, Patty's boss left, and his position was open. Patty was sorry to lose her boss, but she realized immediately that this was a role that could move her career to the next level. This was exactly why she joined this company. But she hesitated, wondering if it was too soon to step up. *What would her colleagues think? Would the senior leaders take her seriously?* She seemed to feel that applying for a job of this magnitude would be "overstepping her bounds."

A week later, she heard the names of three male colleagues who were all in the running for the job. When she sat down with us to talk about it, she said, "If any one of those guys gets the job, then I don't understand it. None of them is as qualified as I am." We encouraged her to step forward to let Richard, the big boss, know she was interested. Patty was still hesitant. She wanted a shot, but continued to wonder if she'd be out of her league running a tax department at such a big company. But she kept thinking about it as she left town for a long weekend in New York with her husband and son.

On the plane to New York, Patty made the decision to throw her hat in the ring. Once her mind was made up, she didn't look back. When she got to her hotel in New York, she quickly emailed Richard, saying she would like to be considered for the job and outlined her reasons why.

The next day, Saturday, Patty, was surprised to get an email from Richard saying that he would like to talk with her on Sunday. Patty replied, "Great, I look forward to talking with you." Then Patty got cold feet. *What in the world am I doing? I don't know if I can do this job. Richard doesn't know me that well. Who do I think I am?*

Patty's husband helped her calm down, and Patty spent Saturday preparing for her phone call.

On Sunday morning, Patty had breakfast in her hotel room. She sent her husband and son out for a walk in Central Park. Then she put on her fuzzy slippers and her warm bathrobe and reviewed her notes. Richard called her promptly at 9:30 A.M., and they talked for an hour. Patty described for Richard the things she had done successfully at her other company and why she thought she was the best person to take on the position. Richard thanked her for taking time for the call on Sunday and said he would get back to her. Patty was elated. As she told us later, "I was just so glad that I had put my name in and had been able to articulate to Richard why I would be the best one for that job. It was a big step for me."

The next week Patty got a call from Richard. Yes, he was offering her the job. Patty said part of her couldn't believe it and part of her expected it. She happily told Richard that she accepted the new leadership position. Despite her initial trepidation, she has performed very well in the job. Ironically, she was the only one who had doubted her ability.

Think Bigger. Aim Higher.

Take time right now to close your eyes and think about yourself and your career. This does not mean thinking about your to-do list. It means thinking about *you*—your strengths, your values, your passions. If you knew you could not fail, what would you want to do in your career? Think bigger ... Aim higher. What are your dreams and aspirations for achievement? How do you want to make an impact on the world as a professional person? If you are like many of the women we coach, you will say to us, "I have no idea what I want to do with my career. I have never really given it a lot of thought." What we will say back to you is, "Well, it's time for you to start thinking about it!"

Remember the old adage, "If you don't know where you are going, any road will take you there." The most important thing you can do for yourself as a professional woman is to determine what it is you want from your career.

As you clarify your ambitions, write them down. You do not have to show them to anyone yet, but document them so that you can see them in black and white. In a couple of weeks, as you become more comfortable with your dreams and aspirations, identify one or two people whom you can trust ... and tell them. Writing down your goals and saying them out loud make your aspirations more concrete.

Next, seek out role models. Unfortunately, even in the twenty-first century, successful executive women are in short supply compared to their male counterparts—but if you look, you'll find that they are out there. Start within your own network of acquaintances and expand out from there. Read biographies and articles about accomplished women in business and government. Find out who the most successful women are in your own community. Google them and learn more about their stories. Find out how each one became comfortable setting ambitious goals for herself and how each one went about achieving her dreams and aspirations.

Just Say No

Doing "women's work" at the office is bad for your confidence and worse for your career.

Are you the office go-to girl for party planning, philanthropic pursuits, office beautification efforts, off-site planning, Earth Day projects, company surveys, and after-work self-defense classes? What about at home? Who cooks dinner, sorts the socks, buys the flowers, folds the towels, steams the carpet, plans the sleepover parties, and buys birthday gifts for your mother-in-law?

We've become lightheaded simply compiling this list. How do you feel, routinely taking responsibility for every little thing? These extra, make-the-office-a-nice-place-to-work jobs are what one of our clients calls "women's work" because it's always the women who agree to take them on.

If you agree to do the domestic work for your company, that's what you'll be known for. And it will come back and bite you. You'll have less time to take on the important business that is more likely to lead to career success. Just stop and count the number of men in your office who step up to plan the holiday party. Why so few? They are too busy volunteering for the assignments that will get them promoted.

Even beyond women's work, it's important to set boundaries. When a colleague asks you to sit in on a meeting or read a report, take a moment to decide if it's work you should do. Without that deliberation, you may find yourself owning work that is someone else's. In some cases, instead of saying no, try to renegotiate the role. In lieu of sitting in on a meeting, should you be presenting at it? Instead of helping a colleague prepare a presentation, suggest someone else who can do it. When all else fails, remember what Nelson Mandela says: "No is a complete sentence."

Be Ruthless with Your Calendar

Now that you have become clear about your career goals and aspirations and you have practiced saying no, you need to look at how you are spending your time. Many of the women we coach volunteer too much of their time to other people and take no strategic steps to further their own careers.

We have a longtime friend, a very successful male executive, who told us that every day, he wakes up and asks himself, *What are the three most important things I need to do today to accomplish my job in a way that furthers my career?* We've found that most male professionals are thinking every single day about what they can do to further their careers and reach their goals. You need to begin to do the same thing.

Here is an assignment. Take out your calendar for the past month and analyze it closely. Use the same analytical skills that you use every day, but this time apply them to your calendar. Ask yourself, *How much time am I spending in a given month on other people's priorities, other people's meetings, other people's development and support?*

We bet you'll be surprised, as our client Alexis was when she did this exercise. She told Jill, her coach, "What I realized was that I was helping everyone else with their priorities. I was going to other people's meetings, and I had an open-door policy with my employees. What this really meant was that my colleagues and staff would come to me with their issues. I would spend time with them, listen to them, give them good advice, and send them on their way. They would be happy, and I would be stuck in my office until all hours doing my real work. This has got to change!"

After you have analyzed your calendar, identify at least two actions you can take to be more purposeful about the way you spend time. (No more open-door policy!) Yes, you can still help other people, but instead of giving them an hour, give them fifteen minutes. Rearrange your calendar so that you have time to do your job in a way that furthers your career!

Take Time to Refuel

Many of our coaching clients are exhausted, not unlike our Superwoman, Jess, whom we profiled at the beginning of this chapter. For us to take center stage in our careers, we need to learn how to manage our energy and refuel for the marathon.

Something as simple as taking regular walks was the answer for one of our clients, who found herself in a very difficult spot. Ann was a type A personality—always wired. She was so high energy that she would crash emotionally. She'd send vitriolic emails to colleagues after hours. She'd occasionally rant in early morning meetings. The worse part of it was that her behavior was starting to overshadow all her good work and put her career in jeopardy. That message came out loud and clear in her 360° feedback. She needed to find a way to calm down and channel her excess energy.

Being the go-getter that she is, Ann got help immediately once she understood the scope of the problem. We coached and guided her on ways to improve her communication style. That helped. But Ann also discovered that what calmed her down was a long walk every night. She and her husband made it a part of their routine. She was able to take regular time out for herself, and it allowed her to better manage her stress.

As Ann's story demonstrates, managing our energy is just as important as managing our time.

Figure out ways to minimize your contact with the people and activities that sap your energy. Obviously, we cannot eliminate all of these encounters in our lives, but we can work to consciously reduce the number of them. Next, schedule two or three ways to refuel your energy every single day. Is it working out? Having lunch with a friend? Reading a novel? Watching a movie? Do whatever works for you. Set aside thirty to sixty minutes each day for "Me Time." Refueling will help you sustain your pace.

Get Famous for Something

A colleague of ours used to say "get famous for something" when he was giving career coaching. He said this over and over again, and he was right. What is your brand? Are you known as someone with

deep technical skills, as someone who can fix projects that are in the
ditch, as someone who makes great sales presentations?

Whatever your passion or expertise entails, being the best (and
best known) for something is one of the fastest ways to gain access
to center stage.

Practice Taking Center Stage

Some of you will be ready to step into the limelight as soon as
you figure out your career goals. If you are, go right ahead. You
know what to do. Others of you may feel awkward and self-
conscious putting yourself on center stage. If that is the case, you
need to find ways to practice. We've talked about the emotional
component of taking center stage, but you also need to consider the
very practical piece of projecting power and confidence once you
actually put yourself out there. Lynne Ford, CEO of ING Individual
Retirement, told us how she worked on her stage presence:

> I probably spent a good five years of my career working on
> presentation skills. Financial services audiences are one of the
> toughest I've ever been in front of. In fact, I recall situations
> early on where gentlemen were reading newspapers in the back
> while I was talking. So I knew I needed to figure out how to
> get their attention and make an impact. It helped me to have a
> mentor who was great at this—and I watched him. He was a
> fantastic presenter: a lot of energy, and he connected with the
> audience like no one else. I learned from him that everything
> was scripted in advance—but he never made it look scripted.
>
> I really got into playing out the scene in my head: seeing
> myself giving the presentation. I found that I had to master the
> content first, and then I focused on the visual presentation. Am
> I standing in one place, am I moving around, am I someone
> who's interesting to look at with lots of energy and motion?

By trial and error I was able to get better. After a while, no one was reading papers anymore at the back of the room.

Being center stage does not come naturally to most of us, even men. They may want you to believe that it does ... but it doesn't.

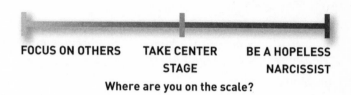

FOCUS ON OTHERS   TAKE CENTER   BE A HOPELESS
STAGE   NARCISSIST

Where are you on the scale?

We're not trying to turn you into a hopeless narcissist. But we do hope that the advice in this chapter helps you move a few steps closer to taking center stage. Small adjustments are all it takes to start the momentum. The idea is to play to your strengths and take simple steps that will help you succeed in the long run.

In order to take center stage, *what New Rules do you need to create for yourself?*

EXECUTIVE SUMMARY

1. Helping everyone around us succeed plays directly to our nurturing instincts, but the inclination can also work against us in situations that require us to focus on ourselves and our own career goals.

2. The Old Rules say *I must take care of everyone else; my needs come last; it's not okay to ask for help; I'm a great number two;* and *I don't belong on center stage.* Give yourself permission to break these rules.

3. Let go of the control impulse. Learn to delegate at work and make arrangements at home if you are stretched too thin.

4. Take time to refuel. In order to take center stage in your career, you need to learn how to manage your energy. In addition, be ruthless in managing your calendar.

5. Get famous for something. Being a go-to person comes with career benefits, including recognition, distinction, and confidence.

6. Practice taking center stage. Find a mentor to watch. Rehearse your presentation skills. Move out of your comfort zone on a regular basis.

4

PROCEED UNTIL APPREHENDED

I have seen her be quite assertive and I know she can do it, but if you have never seen it, she can give you the impression that she is just a nice person.

—360° FEEDBACK FROM AN INTERVIEW WITH A MALE EXECUTIVE

SEEK APPROVAL   PROCEED UNTIL APPREHENDED

Sarah is a talented young attorney we know. Working at a white-glove law firm in the Washington DC area, she had risen quickly through the ranks. The other women who had been hired at the same time had left the firm, so Sarah felt pressure to measure up as one of only a few female partners. Early one morning, both Sarah and her colleague Rich received an email from one of the senior partners at the firm, asking for assistance. *Do either of you have expertise in the area of eminent domain?* The partner was working on a complicated case with one of the firm's largest clients, and he needed someone to help him prepare his legal brief.

Sarah was excited: she had recently written a research memo on this very topic. She acted fast. She sent an email to her manager, asking for permission to assist the senior partner with the assignment.

She got the nod within minutes and was good to go. As she replied to the initial email, explaining that she had just written a research memo on eminent domain and would be thrilled to take the assignment, Rich and the senior partner walked by her office. They were elbow-to-elbow and deep in conversation. Rich already had the job. He had not stopped to ask anyone's permission; he had walked right into the senior partner's office and expressed interest. Rich spent the next month working closely with the firm's senior partner, helping their prized longtime client. He was building a name for himself.

It takes courage to act before getting a green light from your boss, but sometimes you just have to do it. Sarah felt the sting of the missed opportunity, but she managed to learn a difficult lesson about acting decisively and stepping up independently to take the initiative.

What Were We Thinking?

Asking for permission, not making waves, denying our career ambition, doing as we are told, following the rules. These are not punishable offenses, but they do throw a roadblock across our path to power at work. Are the vastly different behaviors exhibited by men and women around ambition a style issue or something else?

One answer is that women are taught to be submissive "nice girls" as children, and it's a habit that many of us carry with us into the office. According to Linda Babcock, professor at Carnegie-Mellon University and coauthor of *Women Don't Ask,* "This reluctance to promote our own interests is not an innate quality or a genetic blind spot in women. As a society, we teach little girls ... that it's not nice or feminine or appropriate for them to focus on what they want and pursue their self-interest—and we don't like it when they do."[1]

Research supports the notion that women who are of age to lead organizations today were socialized in school to be nice—nicer than boys. A study by Diane Reay, professor of education at the University of Cambridge, discovered that teachers and other authority figures in the classroom discouraged assertive behavior in girls but reinforced it in boys. Reay says that the different ways teachers treat each gender support the idea that bad behavior in a girl should be considered a "character defect," whereas in boys it is to be viewed as "a desire to assert themselves."[2]

Despite the damage acting deferential may cause to our careers, some experts argue that we do so because society requires it in order for us to hold on to our feminine identity. According to psychiatrist and Cornell faculty member Anna Fels, "In both the public and private spheres ... women are facing the reality that in order to be seen as feminine, they must relinquish resources—including recognition—to others. It is difficult for women to confront and address the unspoken mandate that they subordinate needs for recognition to those of others—particularly men. The expectation is so deeply rooted in the culture's ideals of femininity that it is largely unconscious."[3] If a woman aggressively pursues her career, therefore, she or others may believe she is failing "to fulfill the feminine role."[4]

It's true that ambition is not a quality that all of us should or must have. Still, if we do aspire to achieve success at the highest levels of corporate leadership, it's necessary that we command the respect of colleagues and shareholders by making the tough calls without second-guessing ourselves. That requires us to reexamine some of our own well-worn rules.

Our Research

In our interviews we thought we would hear that women needed to work on their assertiveness—ask for top clients and important committee assignments. Instead, the executives we interviewed said things like these:

"To be successful she needs to worry less about whether everyone likes her and more about her results."

"She checks in too much. She always wants to know what I think. She gets paid to think! I want her to come to me with solutions, not problems."

"She is a by-the-book person. She needs to grow the rebel in her."

"She comes to me to have career discussions and says she's not sure what she wants to do next. She needs to tell me what she wants to do!"

You can tell by the tone of these remarks that our male bosses often think that we are not strong, decisive leaders.

The Old Rule: Seek Approval

What's holding us back? We've identified some common themes that resonate with the women we coach. These are the Old Rules that stop us from asking for what we deserve and taking the initiative to make things happen in our careers.

THE OLD RULES

1. Being liked is more important than being promoted.
2. Ambition is selfish.
3. I must ask for permission.
4. I'm afraid they'll say no.

Being Liked Is More Important Than Being Promoted

Women are consensus builders. Research shows that bringing people together and managing key relationships are tremendous strengths that women leaders bring to the table. In addition, many of us are pleasers who find creative ways to keep everyone happy. Although these are strengths in today's highly networked world where managing people across continents and cultures is required, they can also be a detriment if we cherish popularity more than results.

In addition to cultural norms and gender stereotypes, we've found two reasons why women feel the need to be liked at work more than men do.

Lack of confidence. Given the ongoing minority status of women at high levels in companies, many of us still feel that we have more to prove than our male counterparts. In the same way that women are more likely to accept the first salary offered, as opposed to negotiating for more money,[5] women feel lucky just to have job opportunities—so we work harder to please and be liked.

Few role models. Directly related to the confidence issue is the fact that there are very few female role models at senior levels in most companies. Our role models growing up—our mothers, grandmothers, teachers, and public and historical figures—may have set a great example in their sphere of influence, but in most cases they were not positioned in the most senior levels of business. This is changing, and our daughters are unlikely to experience the same dynamic we face. But for now, we as women still feel less entitled to go after senior positions and assignments, so we make sure that we're liked and can use our popularity as an asset for advancement.

Ambition Is Selfish

When we show ambition with regard to our careers, it implies that we will focus on activities that direct attention *away* from children and the home. But why is it, even now, that some of us feel guilty about being ambitious? Why keep our desire for success a secret? Fels, author of *Necessary Dreams: Ambition in Women's Changing Lives,* found that "the very women who deplored ambition in reference to their own lives freely admitted to admiring it in men.... Often these women are perplexed and self-doubting as they face painful decisions about their lives."[6]

In our coaching work, we've discovered that many women, particularly working mothers, feel very uncomfortable verbalizing their desire to prioritize work and career advancement as highly as they place family or domestic pursuits. It's easier for men to continue to perceive success outside the home as something that is expected of them. That leaves women, the traditional caregivers, with a heavy burden logistically and psychologically. Despite record levels of advanced education attained by women today and greater opportunity to take on higher-level roles in a business setting, it's difficult to create a work-life blend that allows us to own our ambition.

As a result, some of us still think of ambition as self-centered and narcissistic. If a women puts her career ahead of all else, she feels as if she's being selfish. One woman we work with put it this way: "If I step up and win a spot on the executive team, that role comes with greater prestige and a bigger salary. But it also brings with it assignments that require longer hours and much more travel. I have to decide how much I want those things and how to make them work."

I Must Ask for Permission

We've found that all else being equal, women are more likely than men to ask permission. We'll ask our boss for buy-in before going after a major assignment. We'll take a poll before we put ourselves in a situation that is beyond our comfort zone. But, as Sarah found out, our need to ask permission can put us at a disadvantage.

Asking permission can also be perceived by men as "avoiding responsibility" or an "unwillingness to make the tough decisions." And even beyond the negative perception it creates, our need for approval means that we can't act as quickly as other colleagues who move without hesitation.

I'm Afraid They'll Say No

"Men hear the word 'no' as an invitation to start a conversation. It's a challenge. Women hear 'no' as a dead end. An end to the discussion." A male colleague of ours in the HR field told us this recently. We've worked on this particular issue in the workshops we've conducted with women from various industries, and from what we've seen, his assessment is on target. These are some of the reasons why we women choose to accept no for an answer:

We're efficient. If someone says no to us, we often nod and move on to the next topic or agenda item. Win some, lose some, right? There's no sense in wasting our limited time and energy endlessly debating a topic that may prove to be a lost cause.

We take things personally. It makes us angry to be dismissed or outvoted. A "no" can be embarrassing. It feels easier to bide our time in these cases, to prepare for the next round, rather than to come out swinging when things aren't going our way. We'll wait for a time when the emotions are not so strong.

We like to be liked. As team players and consensus builders, we tend to be the positive force at the table. *Why can't everyone just get along?* If we act like a pit bull, it won't reflect well on us in the long run.

These reasons have merit, of course, but they don't change the fact that accepting a "no" without further debate means we've missed an opportunity to stand up for ourselves and build a reputation for being smart and assertive. We must overcome our fear of hearing "no" and proceed toward our career goals.

Your Turn ...

Take a moment to answer a few questions that may help you assess your readiness to break some of your own rules.

Are you comfortable being the leader and making things happen?

Do you feel the need to ask for permission? When? Why?

Are you ambitious, and if so, is that something that you'll readily admit?

When was the last time you asked to be promoted? For a pay raise? For something else?

What is the story you tell yourself about why you do not proceed until apprehended?

Helen Mets-Morris, a client of ours, is vice president and general manager at Avery Dennison, an office products manufacturer with a presence in sixty countries. Helen is one of the highest-ranking woman at Avery. She is in her forties, very attractive and very British. Helen recently told us a story about the first big success she had as a young executive on the rise.

> My first breakthrough was fifteen years ago. I know it was fifteen years ago because I was nine months pregnant, and it was the first time I actually asked for what I wanted. After four years of studying, I had just finished my MBA in business and finance in night school. That's when a product manager job came open at Avery. Being nine months pregnant, in the back of my mind I was thinking, *Should I go for it or should I not go for it?* But I wanted to get into marketing, and this seemed like the ideal role for me, so I applied for the job.

I filled out my application, but then I received a phone call from one of my friends in the office. Word through the grapevine was that the job was close to being filled. An informal decision had already been made. One gentleman in sales was going to get the marketing role and another gentleman in technical was going to get the sales role. Apparently they'd thought of me, but then someone said something like, "Helen is pregnant and she is going on maternity leave, and we will sort that out when she gets back."

When I heard this, I was so angry that I marched up to the leader of the division and said, "I want this job, but more than that I deserve a fair chance. I want to be interviewed for this job!" This was really the first time that I had ever asked for what I wanted. As a consequence, I was determined to have a good interview.

Well, I really prepared for that interview. I was determined to change their minds, and, after all, I had nothing to lose. I ended up getting the job even though I was nine months pregnant! My big learning was that you've got to ask for what you want. You cannot sit there and expect that the world is going to be fair. That was a big lesson for me, and I've remembered it ever since. I always ask for what I want. I don't always get it, but I always ask.

The New Rule: Proceed Until Apprehended

We like Helen Mets-Morris's story because it drives home a fundamental lesson about assertiveness. It may seem obvious that we need to step forward and lobby for the opportunities we want, but the reality is that many of us expect doors to open based on our hard work and track record. Not so. Mets-Morris learned the lesson early on.

THE NEW RULES

1. Don't wait for permission.
2. Make things happen.
3. Fake it 'til you make it.

Don't Wait for Permission

There are plenty of instances in life when proper protocol entails obeying the rules. However, there are many *other* times when you need to give yourself the green light to proceed.

Being bold and resolute takes practice. The best way to add assertiveness to your repertoire is by looking for opportunities to flex your muscles. Here are some hints to help you proceed until apprehended:

Act like you mean it. It's not just what you say but how you say it that causes people to take your authority seriously. Speak honestly and directly with a minimum of "in my opinion" qualifiers. Keep your voice on an even keel. One of our clients, someone who's worked hard at being assertive, is a pro at owning her ideas. If she's first to propose a plan and then one of her male colleagues takes the credit, she's quick to say, "That's a great idea. By the way, I just said that." She says it without any edge of emotion. Her colleagues have a laugh, and she gets credit for her idea.

Break a few rules. Doing everything by the book is required when you're going to perform CPR or make a perfect soufflé. In business, however, you have some latitude to do things differently. Change-makers and radical thinkers, after all, aren't generally the pushovers in the crowd. So do things your own way once in a while and show people that you are your own person. Watch—you'll gain the admiration of your colleagues.

Be the dissenter. Being assertive means you need to learn to be comfortable delivering bad news or an opposing position. It's acceptable to be the dissenter or to play the devil's advocate as long as you have the ammunition to make a good case. If you can do so in a firm, nonemotional way, people will respect you for it.

Don't overdo it. Assertiveness and aggression are two altogether different things. Being assertive means that you effectively stand up for yourself, your point of view, and your interests. But being labeled overly aggressive, especially as a woman, will have the opposite effect: you'll lose credibility, and colleagues will stop listening.

Make Things Happen

Research on what it takes to be a senior leader points to a number of key competencies. One of the competencies we emphasize in our coaching is the ability to create a vision for change. In fact, when we conduct 360° interviews, we always ask this question: "How would you rate this person on being able to lead change and make things happen?"

The responses are very revealing:

"She needs to lead something that is her own, a big account that she runs and controls. She is usually in a supporting role. She needs to get her own thing."

"She needs to be more assertive. For example, in a senior leadership role, there are hard-nosed decisions to be made and arm twisting to do. I fully believe she can do this, but I haven't seen it so far."

"If change was easy, we could all just snap our fingers. It's not. It is messy, complex, and tiring to make change happen."

"She needs to inspire her team to a new tomorrow."

Many very accomplished women who have made it to midcareer status are not good at managing change. In fact, we recently worked with a group of twenty-one high-potential women whom we coached and trained for eighteen months. The lowest score that each of them had received on their 360° feedback was related to the ability to drive change and make things happen. One of our most difficult assignments for these women was to create a vision for a change and to make a presentation about that vision to the rest of the group. Judging from the group's response after we gave that assignment, you would have thought we had asked each woman to sacrifice her firstborn!

We worked individually with each woman during our coaching sessions to help her figure out a vision for change in her marketplace or office. The idea was for her to articulate her vision in a way that would inspire others. Rehearsals included one-on-one sessions with a speech coach and practice sessions with a video camera to help hone presentation skills. At the final group training session, each woman presented her vision in front of the rest of the group plus some other senior leader. It was a great day. Every one of the twenty-one women presented a passionate, compelling vision for change and convinced the audience of her commitment to lead it.

This "visions for change" exercise exceeded our expectations. As a result of their visions, several of these women were recognized by the CEO and were asked to participate in critical task forces that were tackling tough issues for the company.

Visionary leadership and the ability to drive change do not come easily or naturally to most of us. But as the women in our coaching program learned, leadership skills can be honed and improved. If you want to be viewed as senior leader material, you need to demonstrate that you can inspire others and make change happen. So step out of your comfort zone and rise to the challenge.

Fake It 'til You Make It

Sometimes you just need to take a deep breath and put on your game face. When we interviewed her for this book, Cathy Bessant, the global technology and operations executive for Bank of America, told us how she learned this lesson on the job.

> I was in Florida running a huge part of the bank when the CEO called me and said, "Are you sitting down? I want you to move to headquarters and be the chief marketing officer for the bank." I was shocked. I loved what I was doing and had mixed feelings about taking the job, but it was a promotion and he needed me, so I did it. I was scared to death because I did not know anything about the technical part of marketing.
>
> Once I moved back to North Carolina and took the job, I was very transparent about my lack of ability. In fact I told everybody who would listen that I did not know anything about marketing. In retrospect, I guess I thought I was unworthy to have the job because I did not have the knowledge. As a result, I never behaved with any confidence. I never pondered the transferability of my general management skills. I was trying to live up to everybody else's definition of a great chief marketing officer. I came extremely close to derailing because I was so transparent about my own self-doubts.
>
> Now, this time around as head of global technology and operations for the bank, I won't repeat those mistakes. I have never said to my team, "I don't know anything about this; you are going to have to teach me." What I say instead is, "Let me tell you why I'm here ... why the CEO put me in this job and not a technology expert." I tell them that our problems are business problems, and technology contains many of the solutions. What I am good at is the identification, understanding,

decision making, and execution around business problems. I am good at leading large teams. I am good at making complex things simple, and that is what I am doing here. I deserve to be here.

You know, when guys lose their confidence they just bravado right through it. They puff their chest out and fake it 'til they make it. They do a much better job at this than we women do. But I'm an example of a woman who is learning how.

Cathy Bessant learned from a negative experience that she must appear confident, capable, and focused in order to be an effective leader. You may not be in a position where the stakes are as high as they were for Cathy, but you can learn from her experience. Fake it 'til you make it!

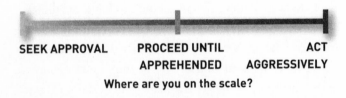

| SEEK APPROVAL | PROCEED UNTIL APPREHENDED | ACT AGGRESSIVELY |

Where are you on the scale?

Being assertive and having enough poise to stand up and lead with confidence require courage. The women we work with every day struggle to find the right balance between being too deferential and too aggressive. It takes a while to figure it out for yourself, but one of the most important takeaways we have for women is to exhibit confidence and take initiative without becoming aggressive in terms of style.

Now, we have given you some guidance about stepping out and being assertive. *What are some New Rules you can create for yourself to make this happen?*

EXECUTIVE SUMMARY

1. Asking permission and deferring to others send signals to colleagues that we are weak or unable to manage power.

2. The Old Rules say that being liked is more important than being promoted, that ambition is selfish, that we must ask for permission before acting, and that we fear hearing the word "no." These are the rules to break.

3. Don't ask for permission — assert yourself. There are plenty of instances in life when proper protocol entails obeying the rules. However, there are many *other* times when you need to give yourself the green light to proceed. Being bold and resolute takes practice.

4. Be the dissenter. Being assertive means being comfortable delivering bad news or an opposing position. It's acceptable to be the dissenter or to play the devil's advocate as long as you have the ammunition to make a good case.

5. Make things happen. Research on what it takes to be a senior leader indicates that the ability to create a vision for change is vital.

6. Fake it 'til you make it. Confidence comes with experience. Sometimes you'll need to take a deep breath and put on your game face.

5

PROJECT PERSONAL POWER

We still think of a powerful man as a born leader and a powerful woman as an anomaly.

—MARGARET ATWOOD

BE MODEST  **PROJECT PERSONAL POWER**

Kerri worked on the Wall Street high wire. When we first met her, she was one of the senior-most people on an elite team of math-savvy quants who spent their time designing financial instruments for high-net-worth investors as well as some medium-size institutional clients. You don't find any slackers in a group like that. Finance top guns, every one of them.

The team leader spot in her department opened up frequently—every few years—because it was a job that often led to bigger projects and more prestigious positions higher up in the organization. After all, if someone was a numbers genius *and* could lead an important team, well, they were golden. Kerri had been a team member for over two years when her dream job opened up.

It was a senior-level team leader spot that involved important responsibilities at the company. The position called for someone with her type of technical background and financial smarts. But she never had the opportunity to apply for the position. She got the wind knocked out of her when the job was given to one of her male peers.

Kerri marched straightaway into her boss John's office to find out what had happened. John seemed surprised—even shocked. He had no idea she wanted to go higher up in the organization. It turns out that doing her job well wasn't quite enough. John's parting words stung. He said she wasn't viewed as having the right "executive profile" to land a bigger job at the company.

Kerri had never shied away from hard work. She did her best to get along with everyone. Her department was making its numbers. She had the functional skills down cold. Yet she didn't have the right *executive profile* to be promoted? It was maddening.

We met Kerri shortly after she lost the promotion. We began a coaching engagement with her and conducted 360° interviews with a number of executives who were senior to Kerri. These were some of their comments:

"Kerri works extremely hard and does a great job where she is; however, she does not interact much with higher-ups. I'd like to see her start thinking about interacting 'up the chain.' She needs to be comfortable with the people in the C suite—the CEO, CFO, and board members."

"Kerri is a great person, I like her a lot, but she always flies under the radar."

"She needs to work on having a more commanding presence. She does not assert her opinion; she usually just floats an idea."

"This is a somewhat nebulous comment, but as meetings break up, there is usually a way that senior executives behave. They engage with each other and have relaxed discussions informally. In fact, this is how they get their agendas moving. I don't see Kerri doing that. I get the sense that she is rushing off to do her email. That is not how a senior executive behaves."

What Were We Thinking?

Taking into account our biological role as nurturers and our propensity for collaboration, it's no surprise that we are willing to share the credit and play down our own accomplishments. In fact, if we feel inclined to discount our accomplishments, as the Old Rules indicate, being modest may be due to self-preservation.

In their book *Through the Labyrinth*, Alice Eagly and Linda Carli say that "people may accept boastfulness in men but, as demonstrated by several studies, they more often dislike boastful women. . . . As a result, self-promoting women risk having less influence than women who are more modest, even though people who self-promote are considered more competent."[1]

It's a classic Catch-22 predicament. If we aggressively advocate for ourselves, we risk being disliked; but if we frequently defer, we are viewed as weak. Regardless of the reasons for this dilemma, the Be Modest rule manifests itself in a variety of ways. We may respond to a compliment or a merit-based award—a pay raise, for example—by expressing gratitude ("Oh, thank you for this opportunity" or "It was nothing"), as if the accolade were a gift instead of something we've worked for and deserve.[2]

This modesty comes with a price tag. According to Linda Babcock and Sara Laschever, authors of *Women Don't Ask*, many women are so glad to receive a job offer that they accept the first offer and fail to negotiate their salaries.[3] They go on to point out that men are more than four times as likely as women to negotiate a first salary.[4]

Beyond the financial drain, there is an emotional toll to be paid when our positive actions are not rewarded. Even when we succeed beyond expectations, some of us fail to internalize our success. The impostor syndrome, for example, a term coined by clinical psychologists Pauline Clance and Suzanne Imes in 1978, is a phenomenon in which people are unable to accept or believe their own accomplishments.[5] We think we are going to be discovered as someone who does not know what she is doing or does not belong.

Interestingly, many successful women fall victim to the impostor syndrome, whereas it is a somewhat rare phenomenon for successful men.[6] According to evolutionary psychologist Satoshi Kanazawa and the editor in chief of *Psychology Today*, Kaja Perina, one reason is that "the definition of success in contemporary society is biased toward males."[7] The authors go on to say, "*Success* in our society is defined in male terms. Nobody recognizes women who are successful in female terms. So part of the problem may be definitional."[8]

More about the impostor syndrome later in this chapter.

Ambiguity also applies to another stereotypically female trait, namely the tendency to apologize. As Deborah Tannen states in her book *You Just Don't Understand*, "There are many ways that women talk that are effective in conversations with other women but appear powerless and self-deprecating in conversations with men. One such pattern is that many women seem to apologize all of the time."[9] According to Tannen, this is more a style difference than a power trap. "There are several dynamics that make women appear to apologize too much.... Women frequently say *I'm sorry* to express sympathy and concern, not apology."[10]

Our Research

Does Kerri's story at the beginning of this chapter surprise you? It didn't surprise us because we've seen it before. We can't tell you how many versions of Kerri's story we have heard over the ten years that we have been coaching high-potential female executives. It is depressing. From our research and from our own years in corporate life, we have observed that when a senior woman does not project an appropriate executive profile, it can derail her career. We have interviewed hundreds of male executives as part of our leadership feedback assessment process. Here are the types of comments they make when they are saying that a woman lacks "an executive profile":

"She does a great job, but she often looks harried."

"It's hard to put into words; all I can tell you is that she just doesn't look the part."

"She's a great individual performer, but she's the type that disappears when she is in a group."

"I can smell fear and so can our clients. I just cannot take a chance on her."

The irony here is that most of the women whom we coach and train are amazing! They are brilliant in so many ways; they have deep professional expertise; they work longer and harder than anyone. They get kudos for turning out great work; however, when it comes to senior leadership roles, men are often reluctant to put these women in the spotlight. The reason they sometimes give is that many of us fail to project personal power. It's a style issue.

Personal power is a unique type of power. The women we coach are all very comfortable with what's known as expert power. Expert power is just what the term implies. It is being an expert in a certain field and knowing your content hands down. Expert power is very valuable, and without it none of you would have gotten as high on the career ladder as you have so far.

A second type of power is position power. We have position power when we know all the ins and outs of the position we occupy in the chain of command, and we exercise that power appropriately and within expectations. All of you are really good at position power; you have shown it again and again over the span of your career.

A third type of power is personal power. Simply put, *personal power is showing up with confidence, poise, and energy*—on the phone, in meetings, giving presentations, interacting with clients, and so on. Male executives consider personal power to be one of the top requirements for senior positions, especially for women. Yes, there is a double standard. We all know senior-level male executives who don't possess much personal power.

A few years ago, one of our clients, a large financial services corporation, engaged us to coach and train a group of twenty-five women who they expected to be candidates for senior-level roles down the road. In the process of designing our program for this group, we interviewed every leader on the executive committee (all males). We asked each of them to describe the leadership competencies that are required of anyone who would be considered a candidate for an executive-level position.

Their answers fell into three categories. One was *a broad knowledge and understanding of the company's business, marketplace, and customers*. The second area was *the ability to inspire and lead leaders*. The third category was interesting: *to exhibit executive stature*. As a result of our interviews, we put together a brief behavioral profile describing executive stature. It looks like this:

Executive Stature

Being confident, poised, and articulate in the following types of situations:

- Board rooms
- Large meetings
- Presentations
- Social functions
- Handling resistance and tough questions
- Speeches
- Off the cuff, impromptu situations

Consistently demonstrating the following:

- Confidence
- Poise
- Emotional control
- Courage
- Patience
- Perseverance
- Ability to manage stress
- Executive presence

This expectation that women leaders must demonstrate executive stature can be complicated. Here is an example: Jill was coaching a high-potential woman named Laura. Laura was an extremely smart analyst with Ivy League credentials. She was considered to be quite successful, a very sharp thinker within her business unit. In the process of giving Laura her 360° feedback, Jill shared the following quote: "Laura does not appear confident in meetings or when giving presentations. She needs to up her game."

Laura looked puzzled and then became very irritated. She said, "I don't know who said this, but they don't know what they are talking about. I am very confident! I know that I am confident." Jill paused for a minute and then replied, "Laura, of course you are confident on the inside, but you are not perceived as confident by those around you. It is this perception gap that you need to address." After Laura calmed down, she agreed to look more closely at how she was showing up. The fact was that she did have some changes to make in her professional behavior.

The Old Rule: Be Modest

It is easy to fall into Old Rule thinking, but once you get feedback, as both Laura and Kerri did, that you don't have the "executive profile" to go higher, you start paying attention to your thinking patterns. Here are some of the most common Old Rules:

THE OLD RULES

1. I feel ambivalent about power.
2. I need to be modest.
3. I feel like an impostor.
4. I don't know how to act powerful.

I Feel Ambivalent About Power

A few years ago, we led a seminar attended by 150 businesswomen. The topic for the morning was "Power: Do Women Really Want It?" Just imagine the noise level when so many smart and engaged female executives divided into small groups and debated the pros and cons of power in the workplace. As the session came to a close, we asked for a tally of how the small groups had answered the question at hand. Their answers were unanimous. Do women really want power? "Yes and no."

Many of these women already held impressive leadership positions in large companies. The others were in the room because they had been identified as high-potentials. Still, they could not fully come to terms with their desire for power. Either they were undecided or they were uncomfortable admitting their dream to become powerful decision makers.

We've already mentioned some of the prevalent societal and cultural stereotypes. Deep down, some of us let ourselves be stymied by the belief that we should still be behind-the-scenes influencers instead of strong deciders. And there are practical reasons that we are ambivalent about power. A scarcity of effective female role models was the reason that topped the list for many of the women that day. The other list topper was plain old exhaustion. If our lives are out of control now, they reason, just add the burden of power, and the entire house of cards will collapse.

Gail Evans, former CNN executive and the author of *Play Like a Man, Win Like a Woman*, gave us something to think about in a conversation we had about the differences in how men and women perceive power. Here's what she said:

> I ask my MBA students, "Who here has power?" The guys'
> hands shoot right up, but the women are more ambivalent.
> One of the guys said he didn't like power because it was too
> much responsibility. I thought that was interesting because the
> women say they don't like power because it is about subjuga-
> tion. Power doesn't happen in a circle. It only happens in a
> pyramid. So it was fascinating how the two different genders
> were both uncomfortable about power for totally different
> reasons.

Regardless of the reasons for their ambivalence, women who aspire to lead must get comfortable with projecting personal power.

I Need to Be Modest

Modesty as a career strategy is overrated. If we hear another smart woman say *It's all in a day's work* or *It was nothing*, we may scream. It's fine to say those things as long as everyone around you knows very well that you're not serious. The danger in not taking credit for your accomplishments is that someone else will gladly step up and do so. We're not saying that it will be a man every time, but you just never know.

In our conversations with women, we've noticed that they've found a variety of ways to fly under the radar. Each one is potentially hazardous to your career.

Being modest. We've covered this. It's naive to believe that your boss, your clients, your colleagues, or even your friends have the time and the patience to recognize your many accomplishments if you continually underplay them. We're not suggesting that you become a bore or a braggart; we're merely advocating assertiveness.

Not asking. We found out later that Kerri never officially put her name on the list for the promotion she wanted so very much. Given her position, she thought it was presumed. This is common. It takes confidence and courage to put yourself out there. It feels personally risky, but there's no other way. By failing to ask for a project, promotion, or raise, you've lost the chance to influence the outcome. You've just given your power away.

According to Babcock and Laschever, women who are less assertive are paid less. "By not negotiating a first salary, an individual stands to lose more than $500,000 by age 60."[11] Another study noted by Babcock and Laschever calculated that women who consistently negotiate their salary increases earn at least $1 million more during their careers than women who don't.[12]

Blending in. Some women go to great lengths to avoid attention. They do not want to stand out—in meetings, in a team setting, in the boardroom. A client from one of our workshops told us that her greatest fear was riding the elevator with the CEO. *What would she say to him? Would they talk about the weather?* Blending in means you may be missing opportunities—large and small—to demonstrate how great you are at your job. We say put on that red power suit and own it. The CEO doesn't want to hear about the weather—she wants to hear about your ideas and accomplishments. So tell her.

Remaining silent. It's not easy to get a word in sometimes, especially when a bunch of colleagues are all fighting for the floor. But failing to express yourself and share your ideas when you have something relevant or valuable to add amounts to yet another missed chance to get in the game.

I Feel Like an Impostor

Gina was accomplished. For three years running, she brought in more business at her start-up firm than any other associate. And she loved to learn. She had one master's degree and was working on a second. If you asked around, you'd find that she was quite a problem solver. When a conflict was brewing with an important customer, she could make it all better. If a technical pricing issue caused chaos, she could find a solution. You just knew that Gina would be running a major company in fifteen years. No two ways about it.

The strange thing about all of this is that Gina constantly felt as though she was about to fail. *At any moment,* she thought, *they'll realize that I'm not as good as they think. They'll know I'm faking it—and that will be the end*. Gina felt like an impostor, and it was weighing her down.

Does this sound familiar? Many of us feel insecure about our accomplishments at one time or another, but in some cases the feeling becomes overwhelming.

In their original work on the topic of impostor syndrome, Pauline Clance and Suzanne Imes note that "despite outstanding academic and professional accomplishments, women who experience the imposter phenomenon persist in believing that they are really not bright and have fooled anyone who thinks otherwise."[13]

Clance and Imes describe the dynamics of the condition and detail the experiences of women they worked with, including one woman who stated, "I was convinced that I would be discovered as a phony when I took my comprehensive doctoral examination. I thought the final test had come. In one way, I was somewhat relieved at this prospect because the pretense would finally be over. I was shocked when my chairman told me that my answers were excellent and that my paper was one of the best he had seen in his entire career."[14]

Although overconfidence may not be entirely beneficial, feeling irrationally insecure will make it impossible to feel comfortable in a position of power.

Cathy Bessant, global technology and operations executive at Bank of America, told us about how she was able to harness her personal power: "My authenticity came out when I separated myself from that scaredy-cat [myself] who thought she was an impostor and who overachieved in an effort to never be found out." She said, "I think I'm light-years better as an executive now than I was five years ago."

I Don't Know How to Act Powerful

Modesty and humility are nice character traits—especially for priests and Sunday school teachers. In an office setting, they can be taken a little too far, particularly if you are trying to present yourself effectively to colleagues and send a signal that you're someone who can handle a senior-level job.

Self-deprecation, wishy-washy inflection, lack of eye contact, and deflecting compliments are all high on the list of power robbers, according to executive coach Marjorie Brody.[15]

We've seen plenty of the power robbers in action. Our client Tina, for example, was a primary offender. She was a serial apologizer, and the acquiescence was never-ending. Finally we had to break the news to Tina that all of her *I'm sorry*s were not helping her career. Luckily, Tina is a quick study; she changed her tone, which did wonders for her reputation. But not all bad habits are so easy to break.

Are You Allowing Any of These Habits to Rob You of Personal Power?

Do you ...

- ☐ Talk about what you are not good at
- ☐ Use qualifying words ("sort of," "kind of," "a little," "I hope I will")
- ☐ Preface statements using qualifiers and preambles ("I am not sure, but ...," "I'm not the expert, but ..."]
- ☐ Overexplain or overapologize

☐ Deflect compliments

☐ Take a long time to get to the point

☐ Ask permission

☐ State your comment as a question ("Don't you think ...?")

☐ Speak too softly

☐ Speak too fast

☐ Have poor eye contact

☐ Have poor posture

☐ Over- or undergesture, repeatedly use or overuse a single gesture

☐ Put your hands in your pockets

☐ Shift your weight to one leg

☐ Cross your arms across your chest

☐ Touch your face

☐ Fiddle with your hair

Source: Adapted from the work of Deborah Tannen as well as Flynn Heath Holt.

Your Turn ...

Once again, take a moment to answer a few questions that may help you assess your readiness to break some of your own rules.

Think of a situation where you were powerful. What did you say and do? What happened?

In which situations do you feel most personally powerful? Why?

When do you feel your power being drained? Why does this happen?

What is the story you tell yourself about not being personally powerful?

As some of the stories earlier in this chapter demonstrate, harnessing our personal power is more important than most of us realize. Exercised properly, it helps demonstrate our ability to handle ourselves in tricky business situations. Handled poorly, it can close doors professionally and set us back.

We'll move on now to explore some of the New Rules that we believe will help you gain a grasp on this important individual asset.

The New Rule: Project Personal Power

Mary Matalin, political consultant and CNN contributor, told us that projecting personal power is all about confidence. "You become the way you behave," she said. We've found that to be true. We use these New Rules to teach our clients to wield their personal power effectively.

THE NEW RULES

1. Exude poise, confidence, and power.
2. Take credit for your hard work.
3. Don't confide your insecurities.
4. Practice your power skills.

Exude Poise, Confidence, and Power

We use video cameras in our coaching and training sessions in order to help individual women see how they come across to others. Most of the women we coach are unanimous in their dislike for this process, but they admit that it is a powerful technique.

Recently, Jill videotaped Joanne, a personable and talented woman who was being considered for a high-level leadership role in her company. Jill asked Joanne to describe the challenges of her job and why she is passionate about what she does. Jill trained the Flip cam on Joanne as she talked for two to three minutes about this topic. Joanne did as she was told and then she and Jill sat down to view the recording. When it was over, Joanne sat in silence for a moment. "My God, I did not realize that I am so vanilla!" she exclaimed. "I was so boring! That was the worst thing I have ever seen." Granted, Joanne may not have performed at her peak with a camera in her face; however, she got the message loud and clear. It was true: she was vanilla, and she was boring. She needed to loosen up, smile more, vary her tone of voice, exhibit her sense of humor, and engage her audience. Jill could have told her all these things, but it would not have had the same impact. To her credit, Joanne took her own feedback to heart, and she's been working on improving her personal power ever since.

Jill shared with Joanne some research that our firm has done on the topic of what are known as confidence markers.[16] These are the behavioral indicators that a person is projecting confidence, poise, and executive presence. Here are a few examples:

Posture. Stands at full height, erect, with back and shoulders straight without being rigid. Chin straight and slightly forward. Weight resting evenly on both feet; feet kept directly under shoulders, projecting an impression of balance and relaxed energy.

Speaking volume. Varies volume as appropriate to intention and content, but stays mostly in the moderate range. Avoids sounding weak or strained. Eradicates any tendency to drop voice at the end of sentences with the last few words trailing inaudibly.

Muscular language. Intensifies statements to make a point. Employs words that are definite, reflecting the speaker's decisiveness. Uses adverbs and phrases that increase or emphasize the certainty of a claim. When offering counsel, uses such phrases as "I recommend" or "I strongly suggest" or "My advice is ..." Avoids empty adjectives and adverbs, such as "interesting," "rather," or "quite." Uses simple language with a wide vocabulary, employing synonyms to ensure that meaning and nuance are conveyed to listeners.

You get the picture. To exude poise, confidence, and power, we have to pay attention to our verbals and our nonverbals. The videotape is like a mirror. Once we see ourselves on tape, we can begin to practice making small changes that will add up to creating a major impact.

Take Credit for Your Hard Work

When Sharon Allen became chairman of Deloitte & Touche USA in 2003, she became not only the highest-ranking woman in the firm's history but also the first woman to hold that role at a leading professional services firm. It's not surprising, then, that Sharon would have some practical wisdom to impart.

During her thirty-five years at Deloitte, where she's spent her entire career to date, Sharon learned some of the same everyday lessons that the rest of us grapple with. As a rising manager in her thirties, for example, she was taken aback when she received a memo announcing the promotion of several close colleagues. She wondered why she didn't make the list. Sharon stewed about it for a day or two and then went in to see her boss.

> Early in my career, I remember being passed over for a promotion. I went to my boss and expressed my surprise. After all,

I had performed very well, and I laid out for him a list of all
of the things I had accomplished. You know what he told me?
That he didn't know I had done all of those things!

When Sharon tells the story today, she laughs and shakes her
head. She said, "That's the very last time I ever let that happen."

Even on-the-rise superperforming women forget that they need
to promote their accomplishments.

Sharon said, "Through my experience, I've realized that many
women think if they work hard, others will recognize their accomplishments and they'll be rewarded. What I've learned is that it's
important to ensure that those around you recognize your accomplishments and the contributions you've made. And there are ways
to do that without being a braggart."

Don't Confide Your Insecurities

Joni was a senior producer working in the media business. She was
an exceptional writer who was able to inspire people through her
email and blog posts. She seemed outwardly self-assured ... until
she stepped in front of an audience to speak. She had a touch of
the impostor syndrome and worried that people would find out
that maybe she was faking it. Stage fright and self-doubt are not
uncommon and can be managed and improved. Joni, however,
couldn't seem to keep her insecurities to herself. Whenever she
needed to make a speech or public appearance, she would tell anyone
who would listen: "I'm a terrible public speaker. I'm so nervous. This
is not going to go well. I hope I do better than last time." And so on.

Her speaking abilities were actually not bad; it was the public
admission of guilt that was the problem. Joni's boss felt that this
behavior was affecting other people's perception of Joni and her
work. He needed her to address the problem before it became a

career stopper. With some coaching, Joni was able to channel her nervous energy in more productive directions. Her loose lips ceased to be a problem, and she even improved her presentation skills.

Grace under pressure is not the easiest thing to achieve. We like to tell our clients to think of a swan gliding across the water: majestic and graceful above the water, but chaotic underneath—pedaling its feet fast and furiously to keep forward momentum. It's fine to feel the chaos, but best to try to display that outward calm.

Bonnie St. John, Olympic champion, motivational speaker, and the author of *Live Your Joy,* is a woman who makes personal power look easy. Here's what she told us about the challenges she's faced being take seriously:

> I'm five-foot-two, so I was the short black young woman coming into the room to present to all these senior executives.
> I told people when I walked into the room I felt like Mickey Mouse: I'm shorter, darker, and cuter than everybody else in the room.... I had to find the inner strength to overcome my "differences" and to be very prepared with my ideas, and with knowledge about their company.... I think part of the training that helped me do this was growing up with a disability, and having people question me about my ability, my strength, my normalcy. I had to learn to look people very directly in the eye and connect with them until they understood who I am.

Practice Your Power Skills

Changing our "natural" ways of behaving can be a challenge; however, learning how to project personal power is a must if we want to succeed at senior levels.

Let us share a success story with you.

We coached Meredith just after she had been promoted and moved to Atlanta to manage an office for a professional services firm. This meant that she would be the managing partner of about twenty-five seasoned partners, most of whom were male and older than she was. It also meant that she would need to run partner meetings on a regular basis. Mary, who was coaching Meredith at the time, conducted a series of telephone interviews with some of the key partners in the office in order to get some 360° feedback for Meredith. As it turned out, the partners had a number of complaints about Meredith:

"She's disorganized in leading the meetings. We never get an agenda ahead of time; she just gives it out at the meeting."

"Meredith is wishy-washy. She always says she wants us to come to consensus. After we have discussed an item, she needs to weigh in and make a decision."

"Meredith may be too young to be in this role."

After Meredith got her 360° feedback, she realized she had a lot of work to do. The fact of the matter was that she had made it to center stage, but she was not performing very well. Slowly she made a number of changes. One of the first she made was to replace her administrative assistant with someone who was more organized and who could help her plan and execute her partner meetings more effectively. She worked with her new assistant to prepare agendas for the meeting and send them out several days ahead of time. Another simple but powerful thing that Meredith did was to subtly change her image. She went to a professional image consultant and bought clothes that made her look more professional (no more dresses without jackets). She also changed her hair and her accessories to look like a woman who should be taken seriously.

Most important, Meredith worked on her language. Her natural tendency was to be informal and spontaneous; however, she realized that these male partners needed more structure and decisiveness from a person in her position. She no longer said, "Hey guys, let's try to get a consensus." She no longer prefaced her statements by saying, "I'm not sure, but a thought I just had is . . ."

After committing to hours of practice and focus, Meredith learned how to project personal power and was taken seriously by her colleagues. Her new and powerful modus operandi gave her a great deal of confidence and was one of the things that helped her succeed in her very big job.

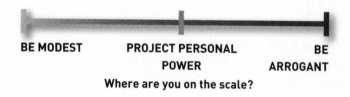

BE MODEST **PROJECT PERSONAL POWER** **BE ARROGANT**

Where are you on the scale?

Like Meredith, you can learn what type of impact you are making on others and make changes to enhance your personal power. We've told you the New Rules we think are important in order for you to do this. *What New Rules do you need to create for yourself?*

EXECUTIVE SUMMARY

1. Our willingness to share credit and play down our accomplishments can diminish our personal power. But it is a double bind: If we aggressively advocate for ourselves, we risk being disliked; if we frequently defer, we are viewed as weak.

2. The Old Rules say, *I feel ambivalent about power; I must be modest; I feel like an impostor;* and *I don't know how to act powerful.* These are the rules to break.

3. Exude poise, confidence, and power. Good posture, a professional image, and a confident manner of speaking can go long way.

4. Take credit for your hard work. One sure way to get passed over for a promotion is by remaining silent about your accomplishments and allowing others to take credit.

5. Don't confide your insecurities. Instead, start from a position of strength by exhibiting confidence.

6. Look for opportunities to practice your power skills.

6

BE POLITICALLY SAVVY

As women, we've learned to rely so much on performance that we lose sight of how important the politics are.

—GAIL EVANS

WORK HARDER  BE POLITICALLY SAVVY

Susan is a brilliant attorney in her midforties. She is a partner at a large consulting company in New York and is known for being a rainmaker. An expert in the telecommunications industry, she has an exceptional twenty-year track record in excellent client service and business development. When we met Susan, we were very impressed with her, even more so when we found out that she was married to another successful lawyer and had three accomplished children. As we got deeper into our coaching relationship with Susan, Jill, her coach, conducted some telephone interviews with key leaders in her company. Jill asked those leaders about Susan's potential to be promoted into senior-level positions in the future. The responses Jill got from the interviews went something like this:

"All of Susan's clients love her! There is no one better at client service; however, Susan never gets involved in the office because she is always out with her clients. I'm not even sure she knows the names of all the senior leaders in our office."

"We gave Susan a performance evaluation recently and we rated her a 2, not a 1. She hit the roof. She was very upset and let us know that she did not like her rating."

"Susan is great with her clients, and she brings in tons of revenue; however, I am not sure that she has a balanced perspective between what the client needs and what our company needs. I think she's got a little more maturing to do."

Jill presented the feedback to Susan during a coaching session. Susan was stunned. She said, "I bring in millions of dollars to this company every year! I can't believe they are complaining about me not being in the office. I thought that selling business was all I needed to do to get to the top. Nobody ever told me there were other things I needed to be doing."

Susan was angry and ready to walk out the door. Jill had a couple of long coaching sessions with her, and Susan finally calmed down. "Well, what do I do now?" she asked. "You need to identify ways to support the company internally and to get yourself better known by your colleagues" was Jill's answer.

It's a common mistake. Susan is like a lot of the women we work with who ignore the need to be politically astute in their work life. They think office politics is dirty and manipulative, and that it undermines the value of good, hard work. "I don't want to be seen as a political player," they tell us.

But this Old Rule thinking is a product of our own self-limiting behavior and beliefs—and it no longer applies. It never applied. Pretending that office politics is not a factor in business is like trying to win the game by sitting on the sidelines. We are not saying be political; we are saying be politically savvy.

What Were We Thinking?

Office politics has gotten a bad rap. To some of us it is a dirty word; yet others seem to understand intuitively that political savvy is the key to the corporate kingdom. It's how business is done.

According to John Eldred, a consultant and professor at the University of Pennsylvania's Wharton School of Management, "Politics is simply how power gets worked out on a practical, day-to-day basis."[1] Eldred, who teaches a course called Mastering Organizational Politics and Power, goes on to say, "People in organizations demonstrate power in every conversation, every decision, and every interaction."[2]

Even if we recognize its utility, Office Politics 101 is not a subject that comes naturally to many of us. In the IT sector, for example, 77 percent of women said they don't feel they have the skills required to manage in a political contest within the workplace.[3]

The truth, according to Lois Frankel, author of *Nice Girls Don't Get the Corner Office,* is that political savvy and the relationships we forge at work are just as instrumental to success as hard work and accomplishments. In her book, Frankel says that women avoid office politics. "We see work as an event where everyone comes together to play nicely. But not only is business a game, it's a game that changes. It has rules, boundaries, winners, and losers. If you're not involved in office politics, you're not playing the game, and, if you're not playing the game, you can't possibly win."[4]

Our dislike for the perceived grittiness of politics may be causing us to miss some important opportunities for advancement. Kathleen Kelley Reardon, author of *The Secret Handshake,* calls politics "a great equalizer" in terms of gender.[5] She states, "While politics is usually seen as a negative aspect of human relations and a low-down dirty means of getting ahead, the politically adept often advance both their company and division goals while doing the same for their own careers. . . . Those who are good at it, whether female or male, have an edge."

Psychologists have noted that some of the distain women feel for office politics may be a result of innate developmental differences and our natural orientation concerning what is right and wrong. In her controversial and landmark book, *In a Different Voice,* Harvard professor Carol Gilligan contrasted women's thinking on morality and ethical alignment with that of men. Through qualitative research, Gilligan asserted that women may be more likely than men to make ethical decisions based on context, attachments, and relationships, bringing our propensity for empathy into play, rather than on rules, logic, and hierarchy.[6]

Leslie, a woman Mary coached some years ago, was a senior leader in a technology company. She was incredibly smart and driven, and she worked harder than anybody. She was on the management committee of the company and had lots of ideas about how to change it and make it better. The feedback Mary received on Leslie was that she presented ideas and then expected others just to come along with her and agree. Her colleagues said she needed to learn the art of influence. She needed to bring people along, take feedback better, and be more politically savvy.

With guidance, Leslie was able to see that she needed to build coalitions with her colleagues. She needed to influence and negotiate to get them to support her ideas and her work. She needed to figure out who her allies were and who her detractors were so that she could work with them to find common ground. A second set of interviews showed that she was learning these lessons. She even said to Mary, "My ideas might be great, but if I can't convince other people they are great, then they are not worth the paper they are written on."

Although one can make the case that distain for politics at work is common, our desire to move into the highest levels of leadership means that we need to leave our disdain behind.

The ace political consultant Mary Matalin wisely told us, "This business about politics at work being sleazy drives me crazy. Virtue can be the essence of politics. The reality is that politics can be just as virtuous or as sleazy as you are. You decide."

Our Research

In our coaching interviews, we've seen consistently that women have a hard time with the question of what it really means to be politically savvy. Most of us are uncomfortable with the overall concept of politics and consider ourselves to be inept at it. These are the well-worn phrases we've recorded over and over again:

"That goes against the grain for me. I am not a political animal. I can't do this."

"I don't think I should have to be political. That's why I picked corporate America and not Washington."

"There is a falseness here, like it is all some game and not for real."

"I won't do this, I never have, and I don't think it is how the business world should have to work."

"This job [firm, company] won't work for me if this kind of behavior is expected."

"Actually, my company does not engage in politics. That's not how we work."

When it comes to politics, the feedback we hear about the women we coach usually is made up of comments about what they are *not* doing:

"She appears not to know how to navigate the firm and influence others to get her ideas accepted."

"If she wants to make it to the top, she needs to understand what it takes. She's plenty smart enough, but can she read between the lines? I haven't seen it."

"She has all of the skills and experiences for promotion, but something is missing. I'm not sure she understands how much of a game this really is."

The reality is that remaining "above the fray" is not an option if you want to rise to the highest levels of an organization.

The Old Rule: Work Harder

These are the common myths and false assumptions that make it easier for the women we know to leave the political game playing to other people. Let's examine each of these myths individually and dissect why developing a new lens for thinking about political skills can offer each of us a few new tools for success.

THE OLD RULES

1. Playing politics is sleazy.
2. I've never been good at office politics.
3. It's possible to opt out of the political game at work.
4. Hard work is enough to get me noticed and promoted.
5. Business should be a meritocracy.

Playing Politics Is Sleazy

There it is again. We're victims of our values, which some people say stress relationships over rules, and nurturing over competition.

We believe that office politics is about winning at all costs—it's not fair and it's not right. Some call it the Old Boys' Club; others view political maneuvering as elitist and dysfunctional. Pure manipulation. But consider what some of us are missing out on by having such a black-and-white perspective.

According to Reardon, women are losing sight of the benefits political skills offer. Closing off our access to quid pro quo at work, for example, leaves us at a distinct disadvantage. "For many women, it's unfeminine to want something in return. That's why a lot of women make themselves available for jobs that men wouldn't touch. Men do favors, but most know and accept that there will come a time when a favor will be expected in return. . . . Many women want to please and be liked, and they do things for these reasons alone."[7]

But there's good news here. Changing our thinking about the good and bad of office politics requires us to use a different lens as we look out at the world of work—but it doesn't require us to throw away our moral code. After all, politics is all about nurturing relationships. When we see a woman who's mastered the art of politics, what we see is someone who's forged a positive line of communication with the decision makers and other influencers in her organization. Politics is about creating a network for yourself and achieving buy-in for your ideas. According to Eldred, "Politics isn't about winning at all costs. It's about maintaining relationships and getting results at the same time."[8]

What's so unfair about that?

In our interview, Cathy Bessant, Bank of America's global technology and operations executive, had this to say about the art of corporate politics:

> Politics is muscle. Men are more comfortable with it because
> it is a muscle. Politics is about understanding sources and
> uses of power. And sometimes it is about understanding your

stakeholders—about engaging with them effectively. To me, the art of politics is about directly contracting and acknowledging the muscle.

Understanding your audience, understanding your stakeholders, is a part of the art of advancing the mission. I think when we fall in the trap of being wishy-washy, we play into the flip side of politics, which is manipulation. To be wheedled into something feels like you have been manipulated, like someone has pulled a fast one on you. By easing into it or trying to be artful about it, we think it won't seem political, but all we're doing is seeming manipulative.

I have had so much more fun in the last several years when I actually figured out that you have to play the political game.

Here is a woman who has come to terms with the political process. She has figured it out.

I Have Never Been Good at Office Politics

The refrain goes something like this. *I guess the political game is just not my strong suit. I'm a straight shooter. I look people in the eye and tell it like it is. I don't play favorites or call in favors. Not me. If there's something to be said, I just put it out there. I don't go behind the scenes to get what I want or deal in quid pro quo.*

Women are not politically astute? Are you sure? Remember the time you called in a favor to get your daughter into a class with the teacher everyone considers a rock star? That was nice political maneuvering. And when you were able to talk that vendor into putting your order at the top of his list and thereby solve your timeline dilemma? That was political savvy. Or when you invited the new neighbors over for brunch ... you know, the ones with the great interior decorator who's impossible to book? Politics—and nicely done, we might add.

Welcome to the real world. We women are *experts* at the mechanics of politics—it's just that we don't always realize it. Looking out for your own self-interests and helping others at the same time comes naturally. Just imagine how much you can achieve if you put your naturally acquired expertise and experience to work in the office!

Gail Evans, former executive at CNN and author of *Play Like a Man, Win Like a Woman,* put it to us this way: "I always laugh when women say 'I don't like to play politics.' People ask me all the time, 'What should we do with our daughters?' I say to teach them how to play chess, poker, Monopoly, Risk, bridge, rummy—whatever the games are, they need to be taught about strategy and bluffing." Look at politics as the game it is . . . maybe you can learn to enjoy it.

It's okay to think of politics as a game if that makes it easier for you. And when you are as good at something as women are at managing relationships and finding ways to be effective, well, it's bound to be fun.

It's Possible to Opt out of the Political Game at Work

It's innocent enough to think you'll leave the game playing to everyone else and simply go about your day. After all, office politics can be exhausting. When would you have time for your day job?

Susan, the high-potential rainmaker we introduced earlier in the chapter, tried to avoid politics by doing her functional job extremely well. But then her bosses told her she hadn't figured out how to succeed in the organization. The moral of the story is this: to some extent, for all of us, politics *is* our day job. In order to do our job well, we need our colleagues—above and below—to make resources available in support of our efforts. We need people to be aware of our skills and accomplishments. We need a network of allies to back us up when the work environment becomes challenging.

Opting out of the dynamics of politics—managing relationships, advocating for our ideas, accepting and asking for favors—seems easier in the very short term. But in order for us to succeed, or even to get anything important accomplished, we need to be politically savvy.

A senior-level woman in finance told us recently of her insight about personal power and politics at work: "I don't really want to be CEO, but the odd thing is that my peers don't believe that. And that turns out to be a really important source of my power. If they thought that I didn't care about being ambitious, I would get marginalized."

It's not possible to opt out of office politics if you want to have a voice. If you want to have impact. If you want to have a career. It's part of the job.

Hard Work Is Enough to Get Me Noticed and Promoted

Many of the women we coach think that hard work alone will get them noticed and appreciated. So they are pure producers—and sometimes they work much harder than everyone else around them. What that insane work ethic gets them is an appreciative pat on the back and then more hard work. They're exhausted. They've built their reputations on slogging through the tough assignments and delivering results. But their herculean efforts don't showcase their strong networks, strategic thinking, or teamwork. And it allows little time for the occasional dose of self-promotion and taking credit for their labor. Hard work, then, is not always smart work when your career is at stake.

Mary played by this Old Rule, and it bit her in the proverbial seat of the pants. She was fifteen years into her career at Time Inc. and waiting for her big break to move closer to the top. For six months she had been coleading a large internal support division. She was splitting the responsibilities with a male colleague who was placed in the division not due to his functional experience but as a favor. It was a good place to park him. Mary was told in no uncertain terms that she was there to make sure the division ran smoothly. At the same time, Mary was asked to take on a task force—one that was fraught with political and logistical land mines. She was doing all this to show the powers that be that nothing was too difficult or dirty for her. She was tough and could make the difficult calls.

A few months later, she returned to her office after presenting her task force findings to management, and found a memo announcing some dozen promotions. This is how she discovered that her male counterpart had been made a VP and she had not.

Mary completely lost it and was ready to quit. How could they do this to her after all she had done for the company? She was not going to take this. Following a sleepless night, she returned to the office to talk to the CEO about his decision. When she sat down across from him, he looked surprised and asked why she was so upset.

Mary told him that she had been running the division for the last six months, doing two jobs. To be passed over for vice president, especially when her counterpart got the nod, was more than she could handle. The CEO said simply, "I never knew you were doing all of those things."

Mary had played the political game all wrong. She had not tooted her own horn and had depended on her boss for that kind of active support. Wrong. She had not built a good relationship with the CEO, who was her boss's boss, so this was their very first conversation about Mary's career. Wrong. She had stayed too quiet for too long on the topic of her division's dysfunctional organizational structure. Wrong. Finally, and clearly, hard work was not enough to get Mary where she wanted to go.

The moral of the story? This disappointing surprise for Mary opened her eyes to the need to be politically savvy and to take charge of her career. Lesson learned.

Business Should Be a Meritocracy

The idea of a meritocracy is clearly an idealized notion of work, but for pure argument's sake, let's say that business can and should operate as such. If we accept that as the goal, then we would nevertheless maintain that politics have an appropriate place. For example, how would one define or measure individual merit without factoring in proficiency in relational dynamics?

If individual merit is based on how successful each of us performs in our day-to-day role, then we need to exhibit a competence in political skills. As long as our definition of politics is one that takes into account its positive aspects—as a means of relating to others, achieving alignment, and building a coalition of people to support ideas—then there is a place in a meritocracy for utilizing political savvy.

That said, business is not fair, and we as women need to be politically astute in order to give ourselves an edge—an edge for succeeding in our everyday roles and an edge for making it to the next level in our careers. As we rise higher in our organizations, there are fewer positions and choice assignments. Political sophistication can be a primary differentiator when a hiring committee is making the choice between two qualified candidates.

Your Turn . . .

Once again, take a moment to answer a few questions that may help you assess your readiness to break some of your own rules.

Do you feel comfortable maneuvering your way through the political structure at the office?

Can you identify how decisions are made and see informal communication patterns across your organization?

Who are the people you need to know and who must know you, so that you may rise through the ranks at work?

What is the story you tell yourself about why you do not spend time on office politics?

Ann Moore, recently retired CEO of Time Inc. and a colleague of Mary's, is a master at this game. Ann was Time Inc.'s first and only female CEO. In a period when media was in the midst of a challenging industry-wide transition, she proved to be a talented leader who achieved a great deal for the company. Ann, having spent over two decades at Time Inc. prior to her eight years in the top spot, was well positioned and highly regarded when her predecessor stepped down. It was known at the time that a new CEO would be appointed. It was clear that there was going to be a race, and several candidates were in the running. Ann, appropriately, was given credit for the rise of *People* magazine in the 1980s and the creation of *In Style*. The informal, behind-the-scenes conversation was all about who would get the nod. Ann had her platform clearly out there: "I am a successful, creative magazine publishing marketer and leader. I grow revenues. I start new magazines. I am going to make this company better than I found it." She carefully continued to nurture her relationships with the appropriate people. It took time and perseverance and a dedication to the process. When the moment came to make the appointment, she was the obvious choice.

Even beyond her accomplishments, Ann saw the value of "running for office," and she did it beautifully and gracefully.

The New Rule: Be Politically Savvy

If maneuvering through the political aspects of your career doesn't come easily to you, don't despair. We'd be willing to bet that even the most savvy women executives, Ann Moore included, had to work at mastering their technique. We can help.

THE NEW RULES

1. Recognize that women excel at politics.

2. Be in the know.

3. Run for office at the office.

4. Become a political activist.

Recognize That Women Excel at Politics

Today and through the ages, women have made their mark outside the business arena. In ancient Egypt, for example, queens governed from around 3000 B.C. Although women heads of state were considered unusual in the modern day before the twenty-first century, in 2010 there were thirty-one female leaders in twenty-eight different countries or territories.[9] As we write this, there are ten female presidents, including in Argentina, Costa Rica, India, Ireland, Liberia, and Switzerland. In addition, there are eleven women prime ministers in such places as Australia, Bangladesh, Croatia, Finland, Germany, and Slovakia.[10] Although we won't assert that gender equity is improving rapidly in many sectors, women are making strides across the globe and flexing their political muscle in government.

Even beyond the Margaret Thatcher and Indira Gandhi political game changers, women have ruled across many aspects of life. Marketers target us regularly because we make the majority of the household buying decisions, for example. According to a Pew Research Center survey, we are the domestic deciders on many fronts. The survey said that in 43 percent of couples, it's the woman who makes decisions in more areas than the man. Men make more of the decisions in only about a quarter (26 percent) of all couples. And about three in ten couples (31 percent) split decision-making responsibilities equally.[11]

Women have proved to be adept at maneuvering in purely political situations, everywhere from philanthropy and small business to family management and local politics. Women, after all, are natural consensus builders who must navigate tricky terrain. When women in our workshops tell us they need remedial work on office politics, we ask them to reflect on the nonbusiness parts of their lives. Managing a family. Being a single mom. Running the household. Making major purchases. Interacting with doctors and care providers. Making elder care decisions. Interacting with teachers and advocating on behalf of children. Creating successful relationships with their spouses.

See for yourself: assemble a list that represents the relationships you manage, the decisions you make on behalf of yourself and others, and all of the everyday negotiations that you accomplish without a second thought. This list should be all that you need to remind yourself that you are naturally effective in political situations. Thinking about how savvy you've been in other contexts can give you the confidence you need to demonstrate political prowess at work. Our point is this: you are a natural.

Be in the Know

Do you know how business is done in your company? Being "in the know" makes office politics much easier to navigate. It may even allow you to have more influence. Here are a few practical tips to help you see which information sources to tap into and what people to count on when you're facing a challenge.

Lose the org chart. Every company is different, but most settings have informal social networks that are just as important as the established corporate hierarchy—if not more so. It's worth your while, therefore, to actually chart the peer groups who have influence. Maybe you've noticed that the movers and shakers all get together informally. Maybe there is a cross section of functional experts who meet monthly to solve difficult problems. Is there a group of young, savvy associates who all head out to happy hour every Thursday? Who are these people, and where are their spheres of influence? Being aware of informal teams and alliances and knowing what each is concerned with will help when you are trying to achieve buy-in or influence a decision.

Connect the dots. Once you've charted the key social networks, map your needs against that structure. You'll be able to use the chart whenever you are trying to build consensus around a particular idea or need. If you require technical support—who are the best people to influence a technology purchasing decision? If you are waiting to receive approval for a new hire—who has a direct line to human resources? When something big is going down—whom within a key network can you trust?

Understand the numbers. Data on the company balance sheet say it all. Which departments are making their numbers this year, and which are in jeopardy? Which initiatives are being funded most heavily? The sooner you feel comfortable eyeballing spread sheets, the sooner you can actually start to read between the line items to determine what's relevant to you.

Get connected. Because things are moving so quickly these days, it's difficult to stop and listen. Often we don't really hear what the people around us are saying unless it has a direct impact on our immediate work. Practice being fully present in meetings and in conversation—you might learn something that can help you. We know one woman who decided to take a different train home each day in order to have informal talk time walking to the station and during the ride. Be purposeful. Figure it out.

Helen Mets-Morris, vice president and general manager at Avery Dennison, told us about the benefits of connecting with people in conversation:

> There's a gentlemen's network that you've got to get into or
> break through. Because we've got to keep doing it every step
> of the way, I've found that one of the important success factors
> is to be informed. I am always up-to-date on what is going on
> in the world of sports. I always know a little bit about foot-
> ball, a little bit about rugby, a little bit about social aspects that
> enable me to engage in conversation. I've seen people's opin-
> ions of me change so many times due to my ability to talk in
> an informed manner about things they are passionate about.
> I think that insight has been helpful to a couple of women that
> I've coached as well.

I was in India and I was with a young female colleague, and we were meeting the people who were building the Formula 1 racetrack. Before we met them, I Googled a couple of the last races. My colleague was saying, "Wow, Helen, it's amazing how much you know about racing." But being able to connect with somebody in a number of different ways is just another part of being a successful leader.

The message here is that you must be strategic to be political, and that requires time and effort.

Run for Office at the Office

We coach women to realize that at a certain point, they need to campaign for their career. It is naive to believe that you will be selected for high-level jobs without making your career aspirations transparent and building support for yourself.

Years ago, Kathryn worked with a former city councilwoman on a city-chartered task force to build low-income housing in their community. They assembled a great team, went through a planning process, and produced a final report. When they were ready to present their proposal to the city council, the savvy councilwoman, who has been involved in politics for a very long time, said, "We need to visit each one of the council members first to go over the report."

Kathryn was concerned about the time it would take to talk with each individual member and wondered why that extra step was needed. "Believe me," the councilwoman said, "this will *save* us time. It is better to hear the concerns now than later in the city council chamber." Kathryn and the councilwoman divided up the task force members and made the rounds. They heard the concerns and were able to factor them into their task force report. When they finally presented the report to the city council, it sailed through.

Not long after that, Kathryn was developing a committee presentation at work. She thought, *I am going to use the lesson the councilwoman taught me and count my votes ahead of time*. Kathryn visited each committee task force member, heard his or her concerns and questions, and factored them into her presentation to the full committee. It worked beautifully. "I am convinced that if I had not counted my votes, I would have had to do it over again, and it would have taken longer." She learned there's value in spending the time to garner support instead of hoping your work is going to simply stand on its own. You need to count your votes.

Here are some of the components of our framework for being politically savvy without selling your soul:

Build a platform. When you have something important to accomplish, you need a point of view. Building a platform at work means prioritizing your goals and creating a formal pitch and message to bring them to life. Be in a position to articulate your ideas and how they map with the larger company goals. Be specific and stay on message. Every time you talk with colleagues or participate on a team, it's an opportunity to bring people on board and bolster your credibility.

Built coalitions. First, identify like-minded people who have goals that are similar to yours, and create a bridge that further links your interests. Second, identify the people who are likely to stand in your way because their interests diverge, and determine if there are ways to create alignment. Think about what sorts of people are missing from your coalition—top executives, technical experts, support staff—and decide whom you'll bring on board to fill the gaps. Finally, identify the people who will never be in a position to support your interests, and consider how to appease them or mitigate the concerns they may raise.

Line up sponsors. A *Harvard Business Review* article written by INSEAD professor Herminia Ibarra and two Catalyst executives suggests that women are mentored just as often as men, but that women need more than mentoring to push them farther in organizations. The article advocates a sponsorship model whereby the mentor goes beyond giving advice to aggressively advocating for career advancement. It reported that "without sponsorship, women not only are less likely than men to be appointed to top roles but may also be more reluctant to go for them."[12] Sponsors expose their protégés to choice assignments and fight to get them promoted.

According to Cathy Bessant of Bank of America, "Without sponsorship, you don't get opportunities. To take center stage, you have to have opportunities. Only sponsorship early on delivers that."

We take sponsorship advice a step further and advocate that women put together their own "board of directors," a group of five or six sponsors. This team of advocates offers you active and strategic support to help you proceed to the next level.

Sponsorship is also one of the many ways that women can help other women. Deloitte's Sharon Allen advises that women recognize their responsibility "not only to elevate themselves, but also to elevate others around them. In doing so, they will elevate their profession. Investors, pensioners and stakeholders are depending on them, their views, their strengths and their independence. Because of what women already have accomplished in business, those entering the workforce are better prepared and will enjoy more opportunity."[13]

Become a Political Activist

In case the message hasn't come through clearly, we'll say it again: you can't opt out of office politics. If you're not sure how to crack your company code, identify someone who seems especially comfortable building coalitions and who is well networked within your company, and interview that person to find out how he or she approaches it.

Working harder to become politically savvy will pay dividends in your career. Take it from Susan. You'll recall that when we left her story earlier, her boss had given her a lower evaluation than she expected, cutting her off from a promotion she felt she deserved.

Over the next few months, Susan and Jill interacted in regular coaching sessions. Susan identified some activities that she could become involved with to help support her company. She began by offering to teach business development techniques to high-potential managers in her office. This was a great way for Susan to share her rainmaker talents with younger associates who were moving up in the organization. In addition to mentoring and training young associates, Susan made sure to participate in conference calls, company off-sites, and a few committees. She made it a point to be in the office more often so she could have some face time with other senior leaders and associates.

One year later, when it came time for Susan to receive her annual evaluation, she was not worried, and, as it turned out, she didn't need to be. She got rated a 1 and received a nice increase in her compensation. She told Jill, "I feel like I have been the poster child for the company this year."

After that, Susan gained even greater momentum. She began to connect with other leaders nationwide in her organization to offer her expertise. She designed and executed a couple of very successful conferences for clients and prospects. She became widely known throughout the company for these activities. Recently, Susan was offered a position as the head of the organization's national telecommunications industry group. Susan was ecstatic. This is what she had been waiting for.

WORK HARDER   BE POLITICALLY SAVVY   BE A
**   RUTHLESS**
**   POLITICIAN**

Where are you on the scale?

Political savvy is not a skill that comes naturally to many of us. The good news is that changing your thinking about politics and realizing that it is an important part of your existing job make it easier to commit to some small adjustments that can have a big impact on your career opportunities.

Career coach Kathryn Mayer put it nicely: "You can be yourself, maintain integrity, and leverage your relationship skills to garner support and recognition of your ideas and advance your career. That's what Political Savvy is all about."[14]

What New Rules do you need to create for yourself in order to be politically savvy?

EXECUTIVE SUMMARY

1. Office politics has gotten a bad rap. Our dislike for the perceived grittiness of politics is causing us to miss some important opportunities for advancement.

2. Here's the thinking that's holding you back: *playing politics goes against my moral code; I am just bad at office politics; it's possible to opt out of the political game at work; hard work is enough to get me noticed and promoted; business should always be fair.*

3. Women—throughout the ages and today—have proven their mettle as master politicians.

4. In any company, information is power. Get to know the formal and informal networks in your office that control the flow of information. Learn to read the balance sheets and what is between the line items. Know how decisions are made and by whom.

5. Think of politics as running for office—build a platform, build coalitions, count your votes, and line up sponsors.

6. You can't opt out of office politics. Consider political savvy as just another functional expectation that you need to hone and master.

7. Call it what you will: building relationships, achieving consensus, networking ... women are good at it.

7

PLAY TO WIN

I think power accrues to those who produce results.
—ANN MOORE, CEO, TIME INC., RECENTLY RETIRED

PLAY IT SAFE  **PLAY TO WIN**

Judy was a very focused and disciplined person. She loved her job. Yes, she consciously broke many of her own rules in order to prepare herself for a bigger role. Yes, she succeeded in getting on the short list for a promotion to the senior ranks. However, when the big boss called Judy to offer her a promotion, he didn't offer her the job she had in mind. He offered her something totally different! Her world was rocked by his phone call. She stuttered and stammered and began to tell him why she was not prepared for the job he had in mind. Luckily, she caught herself after a minute or so and asked if she could call him back. She talked to a few people (including her coach), who helped her realize that (1) the job the big boss was offering was better than the one she had in mind initially, and (2) she had the skills to do most parts of the new job and the capacity to learn the parts that were new to her. Judy called the big boss back and accepted the job with grace and enthusiasm. Bravo!

Suffice it to say, this turn of events would present a major dilemma for most of us. What Judy said she struggled with most in this situation were the risky unknowns. In order to succeed, she would need to put herself *way* out there—manage more people, reach higher revenue goals and sales targets. Where once she managed a small group of professionals, now she would lead a large national sales force. She believed she needed to know how to do 100 percent of the job she was being offered. She did not think of herself as ready to be a leader of such a big group. She was not certain she was comfortable enough with the risk to make this new situation work.

What Were We Thinking?

Judy is not alone. It's normal to feel ambivalent amid major change. Change is risky and takes us out of our element, but these days it is everywhere in business. Success, then, for both women and men, requires a fairly high degree of comfort with change and risk. So how do women fare in regard to mastering this capability? The signals are mixed.

There is clearly a stereotype, one that may have some wind left in its sails, which says that women, in general, are not natural risk takers in most cultures and societies.

Much of the academic and clinical research on the topic is very focused and refers to specific types of behaviors that are unrelated to business. It indicates a higher rate of risk acceptance among men in such activities as driving over the speed limit or gambling, for example, as opposed to taking risks for high-potential career opportunities.

In contrast, a report through the Simmons School of Management, supports the notion that women leaders don't avoid risk at all when it is in service of organizational opportunities.[1] Based on a survey of more than 650 women managers in 2008, the research shows that women consider themselves very able to tolerate risk in order to support a major change initiative at work.

"When you actually unpack the research, the finding that women avoid risk is based on very specific contexts and a limited concept of risk-taking actions," said Simmons professor Sylvia Maxfield, one the authors of the report. It goes on to demonstrate that if one expands the definition of risk to include professional and business opportunities, women are indeed willing to take on substantial risk.[2]

But even the Simmons report on women and risk-taking contained a caveat. It indicated that although women in business do embrace risk, they continue to be perceived in business settings as risk averse. The survey authors attribute this not only to societal perceptions of women as risk averse and but also to a *lack of self-promotion* by women with regard to the risks they've taken and the success they've achieved as a result.[3]

The question as to whether women in particular are truly risk avoiders may be too close and nuanced to call, but the reality is that there is the *perception* of a gender divide. And perception matters. Aside from that, even the boldest among us can benefit from learning how to build smart risk assessment into our portfolio of career skills and promote what risks we have taken.

Our Research

In our research, we have found a theme running through the topic of women and risk. When we asked the question in our interviews, "What would help her get promoted?" the executives we interviewed answered:

"She needs to get out of her comfort zone."
"She needs to put her game face on and get in the game."
"Don't be afraid. Thicken your skin."

"Do not hold back. Let others know what you want to do—we are not mind readers."

"Be bold, take risks, calculated risks. New ideas that work put you on the map."

"Bringing in business will give you power. This is not a nonprofit. It is all about the revenue line."

"She needs to take a chance. She has been in a safe place for too long."

"She needs to be more hungry and aggressive."

We would not have predicted that this theme about being aggressive and taking risk would emerge; however, as we analyzed the interview data, it kept coming up. We heard over and over that women must be bolder, get out of their comfort zone, take risks, and play to win.

The Old Rule: Play It Safe

Who says change is easy? Not us. Before we suggest how to have a healthy and productive relationship with risk, let's first review some of the patterns of operating that we consider Old Rule thinking. This type of mind-set holds women back.

THE OLD RULES

1. I like my comfortable role.
2. I don't like sales.
3. I shrink to fit.
4. I let others take the lead.
5. I might fail.

I Like My Comfortable Role

A little comfort is a good thing. Comfortable routines make us feel safe and allow us to relax. But being *too* comfortable in a job is not necessarily productive. It signals that the challenge is gone, and with it the opportunity to thrive and grow. It may mean that you're *stuck*.

Why is it that we allow ourselves to stay stuck in a job that's going nowhere, even after we've hit a wall in terms of challenge and upward mobility? One reason is that staying put feels emotionally safe. Perhaps we're succeeding—even coasting along—in a current role. Going after something new is risky. It puts the delicate balance of our current life in jeopardy. After all, what if we can't handle all of the demands of the new job? Where would that leave us?

Another reason we stay stuck is a *fear of failure*. Our status in the community, as well as the identity we've built for ourselves, depends on maintaining steady career success. If we try something new and fail, we've set ourselves back in a number of ways. *What will my colleagues think? How will I break the news to my mother?* And so on.

But keep in mind that a comfortable job may not be as "safe" as it seems. If you're not feeling challenged, chances are you're not really firing on all cylinders in any number of ways—in terms of being innovative, for example. When you're not on your toes, there are things that will eventually sneak up on you, such as industry changes and organizational realignments.

Another reason that women stay stuck is a desire to stay put until the job is completed. We think we need to have all projects tied up neatly before we can move on. We say things like, "It will hurt my group" or "I have not finished yet." The reality is that there is never a "good" time to leave, yet moving on might be what's right for your career.

Pam, a client who started her career as an IT professional in the communications industry, is someone who grappled with many of these difficult issues. Although Pam was extremely successful in her corporate environment, she knew that she'd need to make some major changes in order to achieve more in her career. She was getting too comfortable in her job and even feeling complacent. When she was approached by a recruiter and offered a more strategic position at a national consulting firm, she saw that it was exactly the type of job that would challenge her and allow for personal growth. Still, she had strong misgivings. As a large part of her role, Pam would be required to bring in new business—and sales were something she'd never done as an industry executive.

With some targeted training and coaching, Pam was able to rise above her doubt and fear. Instead of continuing in her corporate role and eventually falling into a rut, she was able to see the growth opportunity that the new firm offered. Her positive approach was one of the things that helped her put the risk factors in perspective. She moved from her "safe" and comfortable corporate career to a much riskier job that had a bigger upside. She worried that she would fail, yet she succeeded beyond her wildest dreams. Today, ten years later, she has been promoted several times, and the consulting firm considers her a rainmaker and top leader.

I Don't Like Sales

Not all of us are natural-born rainmakers. Closing deals and bringing in new business require not only contacts but—perhaps more important—confidence. We've found that the art of the deal is something that many very smart women feel uncomfortable cultivating. It's beyond their comfort zone, so it feels risky.

This is an important point because without the ability to sell—yourself, your ideas, your company—it's almost impossible to rise high in the ranks of most organizations. Whether you're comfortable or not, sales is a skill worth developing. We've seen more women than we care to admit back away from jobs that entail persuasion and deal making because they have a negative perception about sales or perhaps about their own skills related to selling.

Some women shy away from selling because they buy into the notion that salespeople are all cheap suits and slick presentations. Women also say to us that they do not like to trade on personal relationships. They say, "How can I ask my friends to help me get into XYZ company?"

But sales, after all, is the lifeblood of most companies. In most cases it's where the growth comes from. You can bet your bonus that the senior management team knows who the rainmakers are in your organization—and they are not just in the sales and marketing department. From our experience, we've seen consistently that women who make it to the top have had sales experience and were good at it. Product developers sell their ideas to secure funding. Managers persuade their teams to achieve company objectives. CEOs bring shareholders on board to support major initiatives. We all need to be good at selling products and ideas.

If a woman perceives sales to be outside her comfort zone, we always beg to differ: women are natural at building long-term trust-based relationships, which are essentially what selling is about. How do we know? We've seen some of the best salespeople in action ... and they are women. What's more, they are women using the skills that come easily to them. After all, selling is about having conversations, attracting interest, using one's passion, gaining trust, and forging relationships. We are great at this!

As the consensus builders, the nurturers of relationships, the well-networked passionate persuaders, we women have all the skills we need to bring in clients, money, and monster deals. Just focus on what comes naturally with relationships, and selling can become easy.

I Shrink to Fit

In the 2010 big-screen adaptation of Clare Boothe Luce's play *The Women,* the character played by Annette Bening, a high-level female executive, says that women "shrink to fit." This line captured our imagination because it illustrates one of our pet peeves: playing it safe by staying neatly within the lines—in other words, feeling obligated to meet the expectations that other people, or perhaps society, set for us. Here are three of the ways we've seen women fall into this trap:

Exhibiting "only" behavior. Many times we women are the *only* woman in the room. It is intimidating. We have observed what we call "only behavior." You are glad to be there; you are unsure about the rules, norms, and unwritten code of behavior, so you are quiet and do not ask questions or make comments. It is *very* smart to get your sea legs before you put any major proposals forward, but don't completely refrain from participating in the conversation or generating ideas simply because you are the only women there.

Staying in the pink ghetto. Inside big corporations, women are overrepresented in human resources, corporate communications, marketing, and other support roles. In fact, each of us has spent time in these fine functional areas during our careers. However, they are not areas that CEOs come from. P&L jobs gain you more stripes and badges than "pink ghetto" jobs, and they have more status.

Doing volunteer work at work. This was introduced in an earlier chapter, but we'll mention it again here because it's a variation on the *playing it safe* theme. For some reason, it seems, the office extras—recruiting, staff development, and organizing charitable giving—always seem to fall to women. Some of you may feel that you can't push back and say, "No way." We respectfully disagree. These are legitimate tasks, yes, and perhaps you feel comfortable managing them. Sure, these can be a way to demonstrate your skills when you are getting your foot in the door. But they do not showcase your leadership abilities. It's far riskier to accept these assignments than it is to turn them down. Say yes too often and you'll be typecast. As one male leader said, "Women can get oversubscribed here."

Only you know if you have fallen into the shrink-to-fit trap, because the depths of personal ambition are unique to each of us. Just know that playing it safe by living up to someone else's expectations of what your career can be will not be satisfying in the long run.

I Let Others Take the Lead

Another way to play it safe is by stepping aside and allowing other people to call the shots or make the tough calls. It may seem safer to let someone at a higher pay grade take the biggest risks, but often it is the big-picture decisions that offer the best opportunity to establish your credibility as a leader. But taking the lead is easier said than done. Some of us fail to step up when the heat is on due to a lack of confidence. It takes nerves of steel to take responsibility in a high-stakes situation.

Gail is a high-potential woman whom Mary coached a few years ago. She was on the succession planning list for several big jobs. She is focused and articulate and has a powerful intellect. When Mary completed the 360° feedback interviews on Gail, one theme that emerged was about deferring. She is not the only high-level woman for whom we have heard this topic come up. Her peers and leaders said, "She needs to get in the fray. Too often other voices overshadow her." They also said, "She is too deferential. She needs to get her point of view across."

In addition to confidence, stepping up also requires vision. Articulating a compelling business case around why you're proposing a major shift or initiative makes it much easier for people to line up behind you.

According to research out of INSEAD, however, the "vision thing" is not something that comes easily to women in business.[4] Having examined the 360° performance feedback on more than twenty-eight hundred women, professors Herminia Ibarra and Otilia Obodaru found that women scored as well as or better than men in several important categories. The exception was vision. In a *Harvard Business Review* article, Ibarra and Obodaru reported that "women score relatively low on key elements of visioning—including the ability to sense opportunities and threats, to set strategic direction and to inspire constituents."[5]

The authors' research includes explanations for the lack of skills related to vision, one of which is a *failure to take credit* for creating vision; this suggests that the shortcoming is partially a matter of perception. In any case, stepping up to take a leadership role, as opposed to letting others take the lead, requires confidence and vision.

I Might Fail

We recently worked with a new group of high-talent women. When we asked them what their career goals were, most said, "I am not sure." We were shocked by their lack of clarity. They had no clear line of sight on their next job. Given that Catalyst research indicates that women are as ambitious as men,[6] we wonder if women are just afraid to say so. Is "ambition" a dirty word for women?

"A lot of women in the U.S. are incredibly ambitious, but they are too embarrassed to admit it," Rosalind Hudnell, the head of diversity and inclusion at Intel, was quoted as saying in *Newsweek*.[7]

Perhaps this is due to fear of failure, or perhaps, as Pat Heim says in her books and speeches, it is a preference women have for flat organizations. Heim argues that women are more at home within horizontal power structures. We eschew hierarchy and, therefore, do not step out from the group to boldly brandish our ambition.[8] Group acceptance trumps revealing our aspirations.

Given the scarcity of women in top spots on the org chart, it's no wonder women prefer flat organizations. Nevertheless, the reality is that success in business still requires women to set themselves apart in top leadership roles. That requires ambition.

Your Turn ...

For you to change your thinking and behavior, you need to have a baseline awareness of your strengths and professional goals. The questions posed here will help get you started.

Are you in a "safe" job? If so, what are your greater ambitions?

Are there instances when your fear of failure held you back from an opportunity?

Think of a time when you took a chance or put yourself out there to sell an idea to colleagues. What happened?

What is the story you tell yourself about why you play it safe?

Gail Evans, former executive at CNN and author of *Play Like a Man, Win Like a Woman*, is a disciple of the Play to Win mind-set. In a recent interview, she told us,

> At the top you have to put your hat in the ring; you've got to actually say I'm willing to play. It's not the covert action—it's the overt action that makes the difference. They are not looking for reluctant debutants in the chairman's office. If you're not willing to put it out there and to fight to get it, then you are sending a subtle message that you're not willing to give up anything for the company.

Evans also acknowledged that playing to win requires certain sacrifices:

> I learned the lesson about not being loved in my very first promotion. There were four of us who were best friends. We all

worked together and all did the same thing. The person who was our boss left, and I got put in the job. I was walking down the hall one day, and the three of them were in somebody's office talking, and when I went by I realized the three of them were talking about me, and it was a devastating moment for me. I realized it would never be the same because I am now the one to determine who gets the raise, who gets what office, who gets what assignment, so it will never be the same. They were never going to love me the same way—and I was okay with that. It's not that you're going to be loved less the higher up you go; it's that you're going to be loved differently.

The New Rule: Play to Win

Gail's story is apt because it acknowledges that success requires bold moves and ambition, but also necessitates trade-offs. Let's look at some of the New Rules that are associated with the Play to Win mind-set.

THE NEW RULES

1. It is a game.
2. Reinvent yourself.
3. Leave your trapeze.
4. Be a risk taker.
5. Be a rainmaker.
6. Do-overs are fine.

It Is a Game

In our coaching, we've found that women think promotions are based on merit. Kathryn was once surprised when a male colleague said to her, "It is a game. You will go crazy if you do not realize that. It is rough and tumble . . . so get in or get out." Truth be told, it is more fun when you realize this. It is a mind-set that women need. Know the end game. Know what winning is. Is it important to have a high score, as in bowling, or a low score, as in golf? Get a clear picture of how to succeed at the game.

Over and over again we advise women to become crystal clear on what specific deliverables signify success. Alexandra is a woman who complained mightily about her recent performance review. Her rating was one level below the top of the scale. When we asked if she had had a discussion with her boss regarding what success looks like, we found that she had not. Had she asked what it takes to get a top ranking? No.

You cannot win unless you have a clear sense of what success is.

Reinvent Yourself

Staying put in a job that's lost all appeal and isn't leading you to better things is riskier than taking a chance on change. The longer you stay put, the more difficult it can be to summon the courage and vision required to tackle what's next. Here's what we remind our clients to consider:

Have a plan. One reason women stay put in a dead-end career is that they haven't outlined a long-term plan for themselves. It's easy to lose sight of your personal goals if you've never identified what they are and committed them to paper. When you create that plan, be specific and descriptive, and revisit or update the plan often.

Look at it this way: you are CEO of You, Inc. Good businesses have a strategic plan—get one for yourself.

Alice is a very bright and competent leader in the risk management sector. She has been promoted several times since joining her organization after college. It is a privately held company, and she is a partner. As Kathryn coached her, it became obvious that Alice wanted the top job eventually. Alice prepared a plan detailing her age and charting which types of jobs she needed to get in order to reach the top. She actually conducted scenario planning on her own career. It was very scientific; it was very methodical; it had some twists and turns and some options. It was incredibly refreshing to find a woman who knew what she wanted and went after it. Alice was not embarrassed by her ambition, and she was being very strategic about what she needed to do to achieve her goals. Alice wasn't so much reinventing herself as she was *inventing* herself.

Get a posse. In addition to a plan, reinvention requires an army of supporters. Having friends, connections, and sponsors throughout your industry—and beyond it—makes getting unstuck much easier. These people are not only your lifeline but also your eyes and ears out in the wider world of work. When you are ready to make a move, you'll be glad you cultivated support.

Get past the impasse. According to Timothy Butler, reaching a dead end personally or professionally can be stressful and painful—but it is a necessary step to clearing the impasse and arriving at a new and better place. "When we have run aground, we sometimes fail to realize that this is a necessary crisis, without which we cannot grow, change and—eventually—live more fully in a larger world," Butler explains in his book *Getting Unstuck*. He goes on to offer a six-phase process for "imagining a new place in life and taking the leap to get there."[9]

These crises are almost always good things because they are wake-up calls. Louise, a woman Jill coached, once said, "My goodness, if my career hadn't stalled I wouldn't have taken the time to figure out what makes me happy and what I really want to do!"

Make a major change. Although you'll want to be able to leverage your hard-earned experience and competencies, as well as your network, don't be afraid to make a radical change if that's what's required to achieve your personal and professional goals. After all, our objectives sometimes change midcareer. Perhaps an entrepreneurial endeavor is more appealing than a corporate job and better suits your needs? All three of us left jobs in corporate America and started our own business. It has been exciting to learn new skills—skills we hardly knew that we had.

Lynne Ford, CEO of ING Individual Retirement, told us, "You know that old adage: if you do not like your friends, get new ones; there are lots of people out there who can be your friend." She said that the same thing is true about a job. There are lots of jobs out there. If you do not like your job, get a new one.

In *Working Identity,* her book about reinventing yourself and your career, Herminia Ibarra says that major career transitions take three to five years and can be messy and nonlinear. There is no one perfect career waiting to be discovered, she says, but instead there are many possible selves we can become. She goes on to say that finding the one that fits is the result of doing and experimenting—trying on possibilities through a process of trial and error.[10]

Consider perception. Helen Mets-Morris, vice president and general manager of Avery Dennison, told us what she learned about personal power and perception:

Very recently my feedback from my boss was "Helen,
often a person's first impression of you is that you are

young, attractive, and nice ... but it takes them a couple
of interactions to realize that you're also very smart." That
really had an impact on me. I've worked on being far more
intentional about my impact. Going into a meeting, I am
aware of my agenda, what the challenge in the meeting will be,
and I'm deliberate about how I want to be perceived.

Leave Your Trapeze

The American futurist Marilyn Ferguson said, "It is not so much that
we're afraid of change or so in love with the old ways, but it's that
place in between that we fear. It's like being between trapezes. It's
Linus when his blanket is in the dryer. There's nothing to hold on to."

There comes a time for each of us when playing it safe just
won't get the job done. Maybe you're competing for the job of your
dreams. Perhaps you have a new product idea that's so bold and
audacious the possibilities are keeping you awake at night. It could
be that you are simply frustrated by the status quo and are finally
ready to make a radical change. Regardless of the specific reason for
change, now is the time to let go of your fear and take a leap into
the great unknown.

If you aren't a natural risk taker or don't like putting yourself
out there, here is our advice to help you leave your trapeze:

Get a new mantra. We're not suggesting that you listen to hours
of motivational tapes or any such thing. Still, you need to prepare
your mind and get your competitive juices flowing. One great way
to do that is by giving yourself a pep talk. In fact, we even suggest
that you have a personal mantra or affirmation (for example, *This is
my time* or *This promotion is mine*). This phrase—to be remembered
and repeated—will help you envision achieving your goal. Seriously,
give it a chance, and you'll see that it keeps you focused and gives
you strength.

Have a vision. We keep coming back to this. Before you take a major risk and go after something big, it's important to formulate a clear vision of what success looks like. Close your eyes and imagine being successful with the risk you are taking. Having that picture in mind will not only focus you on the finish but also help you articulate the intermediate steps that will get you there. It is important to be able to describe success. If you were successful, what would people be saying? What would be happening? Your vision will help you create a pitch to bring colleagues on board in service of your objectives.

Just do it. Try not to overthink things. Sometimes—and you'll know when those times are—it's best to simply step up and take a swing. Have that vision in your mind. Think about your mantra. And take the leap. This is what we call a Hokey-Pokey moment. Put your whole self in.

Be a Risk Taker

Becoming comfortable with risk and change is one thing. Actually leading the change is quite another. Still, if you are frustrated with the inefficiencies you see all around you, why not take the initiative and improve the situation? It's a great way to establish yourself as a leader and a problem solver.

Our client Ellen was an operations officer who became concerned when customers were complaining about the repetitive paperwork required to buy more than one service at her bank's branches. She ran the problem up the flagpole but didn't hear back. Marketing passed the problem over to customer relations. Customer relations brought IT in the loop. IT sent it over to compliance. Compliance passed it right back to Ellen.

After some analysis, Ellen discovered that it required seventeen different forms for a customer to open a routine checking account and savings account, receive overdraft protection, and request an ATM card. This was ridiculous. She decided to find a way to change the process and fix the problem herself. Ellen worked diligently across departments, reached out and twisted some arms, used all her creativity, and unleashed skills of persuasion she didn't even know she had. Finally, after several months of effort, she created a *single form* that customers could fill out to open all of these services. Not only were the bank's customers delighted, but Ellen's efforts also saved the bank in excess of $300,000 annually on just the forms alone! No one had asked her to this—she took a risk.

Driving change requires time and persistence—not to mention a strong vision. As Ellen learned, it's worth the effort. She not only saved money and vastly improved a fundamental process but also made a name for herself throughout the company as a leader, problem solver, and change agent.

In an interview, Helen Mets-Morris of Avery Dennison told us her perspective on risk: "I am a risk taker. If you spoke to people who work for me, I think they could list four or five big risks that I've taken in the last year, including presenting a restructuring of my own role to reorganize business around market segmentation." Mets-Morris went on to tell us why women have an edge when it comes to risk. "The farther you go up the career ladder, the bigger the decisions are that you have to make—so the risks and opportunities become bigger as well. I'll always have somebody on my right-hand side checking through the data, but for me what's important is relying on my intuition. That is an element where females have an advantage—our internal intuition."

Be a Rainmaker

Women who can sell are powerful. There's no two ways about it. As we mentioned earlier in the chapter, rainmakers get

promoted. Why? Because they bring in business! And you don't
need to be on the sales team to be a rainmaker. If you are managing
client relationships, closing deals of any sort, or even managing a
team of customer-facing contributors—you can use your skills
to become visible by bringing revenue and customers into the
organization. Julie Morgenstern, author of the book *Never
Check Email in the Morning,* says, "Dance close to the revenue
line."[11]

We recently met a woman who targeted a Fortune 100 company, won the work, and has grown the revenue from the client to
$300 million. She said, "My company is paying a lot of attention to
me." Surprise, surprise.

In our experience, we've found that a few simple rules of
thumb can help you bring in new business for your organization.
First, selling is about cultivating relationships. As in negotiation,
it is important that both sides perceive the transaction as being
transparent and fair. Second, the more that you can demonstrate
genuine passion (for what you and your organization are selling),
the more you'll be able to gain the trust of clients and customers.
Selling is about trust and authenticity.

Women are outstanding at this!

Do-Overs Are Fine

As Thomas Edison famously said, "I have not failed. I've just
found 10,000 ways that won't work." The case we've been making
throughout this chapter is that it's far riskier to hold back than it
is to put yourself out there and play to win. Of course, the reason
many of us hold back is that we're afraid of what failure will bring.
It's embarrassing, disappointing, and costly.

There's more than one way to snatch a slice of victory from
defeat.

A great method for changing your perspective on failure is to think like an entrepreneur. Because most start-ups sink, the vast majority of serious entrepreneurs fail multiple times before they succeed. Every failure—if handled appropriately—is viewed as another step closer to success. In fact, venture capitalists rarely hire a CEO who hasn't crashed and burned at least once. A taste of failure is considered valuable experience!

The truth is that nearly every wildly successful CEO or business builder has failed sometime in his or her past. Bill Gates launched a business failure prior to Microsoft. Oprah Winfrey was fired from an early television job before shooting to stardom and success. Steve Jobs and Apple introduced a PDA you've never heard of, called the Newton. It was a colossal failure. Colonel Sanders failed mightily before succeeding with Kentucky Fried Chicken.

The important feature of failure is the ability to learn from your mistakes and to pick yourself up to start again. In many cases, do-overs are fine, because past experience makes you smarter. Great managers instill this value in their people.

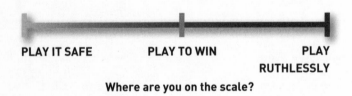

PLAY IT SAFE   PLAY TO WIN   PLAY RUTHLESSLY

Where are you on the scale?

Success is about taking calculated risks. Some organizations have a much higher tolerance for risk-taking than others do. And like organizations, some of us are born rainmakers in the purest sense, whereas others persuade and manage change by deftly cultivating close relationships. Regardless, it's important to know where you are on the scale and be ready to move farther over to the right side when a great idea or opportunity presents itself. We are not suggesting that you should act ruthlessly ... just go for the win!

We've given you some new rules to help get you started. *What New Rules do you need to create for yourself?*

EXECUTIVE SUMMARY

1. A comfortable job may not be as "safe" as it seems. If you're not feeling challenged, chances are you're not really firing on all cylinders.

2. These are patterns of thinking that can block our path to power: *I'll stay in my comfortable role; I don't like sales; I shrink to fit; I let others take the lead;* and *I might fail.*

3. Without the ability to sell—yourself, your ideas, your company—it's almost impossible to rise high in the ranks of most organizations. Whether you're comfortable or not, sales is a skill worth developing.

4. As the consensus builders, the nurturers of relationships, the well-networked passionate persuaders, women have all of the skills we need to bring in clients, money, and major deals.

5. It may seem safer to let someone at a higher pay grade take the big risks, but often it is the big-picture decisions that offer the best opportunities to establish your credibility as a leader.

6. Leave your trapeze by preparing your mind, having a vision, leaving room for improvisation, and trying not to overthink things.

7. It's important to learn from your failures. One great way to change your perspective on failure is to think like an entrepreneur.

8

IT'S BOTH-AND

The equation to solve for is happiness with the least amount of guilt.
There are no right answers here.

—SUSAN IVEY, CEO OF REYNOLDS AMERICAN, RECENTLY RETIRED

IT'S ALL OR
NOTHING

IT'S BOTH-AND

Allison drove herself hard for her success. As the brand management executive for a consumer products company, she was "on call" at all hours of the day and night—always ready to talk with board members, outside retail buyers, and the various product developers and sales directors. There were fires to put out and decisions to be made. There were early morning breakfast meetings, after-work drinks with retailers, and even weekend-long pitch meetings. She had high expectations for herself and everyone around her.

Life in the fast lane was exactly what she had signed up for. To Allison, the perks of power were well worth the sacrifice. Traveling was her favorite pastime. She was on the road for several days every week. Her job title was a status symbol in her social network. And she was one-half of a power couple: her husband worked even longer hours than she did. He'd made partner in record time at a brand-name management consulting firm. Work was their life, and Allison couldn't imagine any other lifestyle.

So why did Allison come so close to walking away?

It happened when she received some surprising and disappointing news. It was the usual story: she lost a promotion that she felt she unquestionably deserved. The CEO brought in someone else to fill the executive slot she had been gunning for. Without skipping a beat, she called a friend who is a headhunter and told her she was updating her resume. *Get me out of here*, she said. She was angry and emotional: ready to leave behind the perks she loved, the colleagues she considered family, and a salary that was pretty extraordinary. The burnout that she'd kept at bay for a while now was starting to show.

After Allison had taken a few days off, one of her mentors was able to talk her off the ledge. *Did she realize what she would be walking away from?* Her husband, too, encouraged her to go back and figure out what had happened. So Allison sat down with her CEO and shared her disappointment. She asked what she could have done to win the role. *Wasn't she already giving everything to the job?* she wondered.

Part of the problem, he told her, was that she saw everything in black and white. She had a difficult time listening to opposing perspectives. Apparently some of her peers had complained about her demanding style and "my way or the highway" attitude. Given that their industry was in a state of constant change, the CEO was looking for her to demonstrate that she could deal with ambiguity. He reminded her, *Leadership is about people's goals and desires; it's about the market and the economics of a business. There are so many factors. Allison, it is not about being perfect. There is always more than one answer, not one perfect way.* These were the same things he'd been telling her for years in their performance discussions. He did not want to lose her, but she had some work to do if she wanted to land the next-level big job.

Allison's reaction to disappointment was indicative of her extreme style. Her all-or-nothing demeanor had been a net positive so far in terms of career advancement, but her tendency toward black-and-white, perfectionist thinking was working against her. She didn't seem to be able to grasp that there could be two "rights." This is about the time we started working with Allison. It was difficult for her to hear the negative feedback, but the experience made her realize that she needed to get her life in perspective. And, as always, she put her whole self into it.

It's easy to fly off the handle and walk away when the going gets tough, but it's seldom the right move. The ability to deal with disappointment and frustration and remain calm amid the constant change has become a skill that leaders need to master.

What Were We Thinking?

Business is changing faster than ever before, making resilience a primary leadership trait. This is not exclusively a women's issue—dealing with uncertainty and ambiguity is no easy feat for anyone. Although extreme behavior, such as perfectionism, can be a conduit for ambition, studies indicate that it also leads to dissatisfaction and burnout. Susan Ivey, who recently retired as CEO of Reynolds American, said to us, "We women develop this superhero mentality that we have to be able to do it all, that we need to know it all and have all the answers."

Professor Cary Cooper, an expert in organizational psychology and health at Lancaster University, said women are negatively affected when they can't live up to their extreme need to achieve. They "feel guilty that they're not doing well at work because of home commitments and they're not doing well at home because of work commitments." He added, "Women suffer from perfectionism. They tend to be more conscientious, working to 100%."[1]

A 2008 study of 288 adults, published in the *Journal of Occupational and Organizational Psychology*, found that a higher proportion of women felt they did not meet their own very high standards when it came to work and family commitments.[2] It went on to conclude that perfectionism in women had a negative impact on work-life balance.

Further, data released by the General Social Survey (GSS) show that women's satisfaction has been on a downward trend since the 1970s.[3] One way to interpret this report is to attribute this decline in happiness partially to a disconnect between women's high aspirations and their attainment. Women expect more and have extreme expectations for their lives compared to men, so they are more disappointed if they do not attain all that they hope. Does that sound familiar? It does to us. Many of the women we coach struggle with the trade-offs associated with needing to *have it all*.

In *Find Your Strongest Life: What the Happiest and Most Successful Women Do Differently*, the "find your strengths" expert Marcus Buckingham says that better education, better jobs, and better pay have simply not resulted in fulfillment across the board for women in recent decades. Buckingham concludes that women should quit looking for the perfect balance of all things; they should instead focus on whatever specific things will make them the happiest.[4]

Striving for perfection is not only hard on us as individuals; it can also have a negative impact on our performance as leaders. Experts say that it is difficult to work for perfectionist bosses because they have unreasonable expectations of employees.[5]

All of us fall victim to the desire for perfection at one time or another. Kathryn had one such moment that she recalls very vividly:

> I was working for the bank years ago when my two children were in middle school. Running errands was always very difficult with a full-time job. One weekday I needed to get to the shoe repair shop to pick up my son's shoes for him to wear to his first big teenage party that Saturday. On both Wednesday and Thursday, I planned to leave work early to pick up the shoes, but each time I stopped to talk to somebody, answer one more phone call, send one more email . . . and two days in a row I got to the shoe repair shop after it closed. On Friday, I made sure that I left in plenty of time. I wasn't going to miss picking up the shoes for the third time. I left the office with time to spare and got in my car headed to pick up the shoes; however, to my distress, I found myself caught in a horrible traffic jam. You know what happened. The shoe repair shop was shuttered when I arrived.
>
> Sitting in my car in the parking lot I burst into tears. I didn't just cry, I sobbed. *I am a terrible mother. Why did I think I could make this all work? I can't be a good mother* and *be good at my job. Hell, I can't even manage to pick up a pair of shoes!*
>
> When I got home, I called a dear friend and told her what happened. She listened intently and then said, "Don't you think you are overreacting just a little bit? . . . It seems like your thinking is off on this." She was right. My meltdown was really all about my need for perfection.

This is an example of all-or-nothing thinking: *Either I'm a good mother and can find time to pick up my son's shoes or I'm a bad mother because I can't get to the shoe repair shop before it closes.* Picking up shoes, of course, is not what really counts in motherhood. No matter our family status, we all have moments when we hit a wall dealing with our complicated, overfilled lives. Sometimes an experience like this can motivate us to make changes and move forward, but sometimes it causes us to make an extreme choice about our careers that we might later regret.

Our Research

In our interviews, we witnessed the emergence of a clear and overwhelming theme. It did not matter if the executive we interviewed was talking about a woman who was single or married, who had children or no children; the topic of life as an *all-or-nothing proposition* dominated the interview feedback.

"She does not deal well with ambiguity. She does not see the gray."
"She needs to learn to let things go sometimes."
"She is going to burn out unless she figures out her work-life mix. She takes criticism way too hard."
"She drives herself and those around her so hard that she runs out of gas and so do they."
"She seeks perfection in everything she does and then runs out of steam."

In our coaching sessions, women tell us:

"I cannot seem to get it all right. Something is always crashing."
"I feel guilty. The guilt is like a yoke around my neck."
"If this company asks me to do one more thing, I'll quit."
"I cannot allow any work to go out of here that is not an 'A.' "

This tendency to believe that we need to do it all—and to feel like a failure when we realize it's impossible—may emerge from the stress of our busy lives. Or perhaps it is a result of the unrealistic expectations we've set for ourselves and others. Regardless of the source, this distorted thinking is harmful.

The Old Rule: It's All or Nothing

The "all-or-nothing" trap robs us of satisfaction and success. Luckily, it is a great place to start to break your own rules. Success looks different to each of us, however, so it's up to you to figure out creative solutions for yourself. Here are a few of the Old Rules for you to examine.

THE OLD RULES

1. I'm prone to negative thinking.
2. Everything is black and white.
3. Success means doing it all.
4. I'll opt out.

I'm Prone to Negative Thinking

According to Davis Burns, author of *The Feeling Good Handbook,* extreme thinking can lead to depression and anxiety. Certain specific exaggerated or irrational thought patterns, called "cognitive distortions," are the culprits that reinforce harmful emotions and get in our way.[6] The box "Irrational Thinking" lists a few of the negative thinking patterns that keep us feeling bad about ourselves.

IRRATIONAL THINKING

All-or-nothing thinking. We see things in absolute, black-and-white terms. As we've mentioned, this type of thinking causes us to feel the sting of failure unless we are entirely perfect.

Overgeneralization. One small setback causes us to feel that all is lost. "I flubbed the presentation today, so my career is finished." We see a single negative event as total defeat.

Mental filters. We pick out one negative detail and focus on it to the exclusion of all else. Imagine that you just received a promotion and pay raise, but your new job title is not what you were hoping for—and that's all you can think about. This type of preoccupation blocks out the positive details associated with a situation.

Disqualifying the positive. We discount or filter out positive experiences by insisting that they don't count. This leaves room for only negative thinking.

Personalization. We see ourselves as the primary cause of negative events that are not in fact our fault. If we lose a client as a consequence of poor economic conditions, for example, we may blame the loss on a perceived shortcoming of our own.

Source: Adapted from David D. Burns, *The Feeling Good Handbook* (New York: Morrow, 1989), 8–11.

We see this type of thinking in our work with professional women. Mandy, a woman Jill coached a few years back, is someone who comes to mind. Judging by her 360° feedback, Mandy was very well regarded. Her colleagues, peers, and even a few members of the executive committee had commented on her excellent work. Among other positive feedback, they said she was responsible for improving processes, hiring talented people, and growing revenue for the group. To Jill's surprise, Mandy was highly concerned about the one bit of developmental advice she received in the interviews. Her peers had said she needed to let go of the detail work, that she got too much into the weeds.

Mandy was positively fixated on this one shred of constructive feedback. She felt that she was failing at her job. She was a miserable manager and an utter failure. Although Jill worked with her to help her see the feedback in the proper light, it was difficult for Mandy to keep it in perspective and see it for what it really was: one piece of developmental advice in an otherwise glowing feedback report.

Everything Is Black and White

There's no one right way to succeed, but refusing to be flexible is a sure way to fail. Black-and-white thinking prevents you from finding the middle ground. We know—shades of gray are not as bold and exciting as black and white, but inflexible thinking can hurt relationships and also cause you to miss opportunities. Here are some of the warning signs that you are not seeing the gray zone:

You get locked in. Most professions and industries are in transition right now—business models are changing faster than shoe styles. A refusal to consider alternatives means you may fail to anticipate a major wave of business change. This is what Allison's boss was concerned about. The most successful women leaders we know are flexible enough to deal with complex situations that don't have concrete answers.

Dealing with complex situations requires a willingness to take leaps and be innovative. If the first solution you come up with doesn't cut it, make a fast course correction and settle on a plan B. This type of flexible thinking doesn't leave room for going to extremes. In her book *Influencing with Integrity,* Genie Laborde says, "The person with the most flexibility has the most power."[7]

You micromanage. There is more than one way to do almost anything. Managers who suffer from black-and-white thinking drive their teams to distraction because they can't bear to see their rigid plans altered. (It's my way or the highway.) Assuming that no major rules are being broken, manage the end goal rather than dictate the exact route a colleague should take to get there.

You don't see the gray areas. Most times there's no clear right or wrong answer to a problem or question. If we have an inflexible attachment to our perspective, we're usually making decisions based on some of the facts but not all. As difficult as it may seem, sometimes we have to hold two opposing ideas in our minds at the same time in order to remain flexible.

Susan Ivey, the recently retired CEO of Reynolds American, put it this way to us: "You have to be able to live in gray. Women believe they have to figure it all out and have all the answers. But in order to know which way to go in business, you have to recognize when it is gray and have the ability to visualize other perspectives."

Success Means Doing It All

Many of us remember the famous Enjoli perfume commercial with the gorgeous and energetic career woman strutting in from work in her silk dress and shimmying around the kitchen to the "I can bring home the bacon, fry it up in the pan" song. And who wouldn't want to be her? But she represented an impossible ideal.

The author and journalist Gloria Steinem told a group of clinicians at their 2009 annual meeting that women still believe the dangerous myth that they can be superwoman: "Women are told they can have it all, that they can do anything ... as long as they also keep doing everything else they were doing before."[8]

Steinem was making the point that society perpetuates the drive for perfection and superachievement. We've seen it many times in our coaching work: women set themselves up for failure by striving to do it all and make it look easy. We've seen women who end up in the hospital because they think they should be able to have a high-pressure job and a high-demand family—and manage everything without any help or accommodation. That's a lot to expect. It's unrealistic and unfair to place those demands on yourself.

The problem with setting impossibly high goals for ourselves is how we feel when we can't achieve them: demoralized and disappointed. Perhaps it's time to get real and give ourselves a break. Although society may deserve some of the blame for our burning desire for high achievement as well as perfect nails, the reality is that we're the only ones who can fix the problem.

When we interviewed Mary Matalin, political consultant and CNN contributor, she put it this way: "As women we think we can't take time to take care of ourselves. But if we don't take care of ourselves first, we can't help anybody else. Put on your own oxygen mask first. If you can't find a way to put yourself first, then you can't function. A little bit goes a long way."

Set priorities around what makes you feel most fulfilled and have realistic goals that you can build on.

I'll Opt Out

There are a variety of reasons why women, including women we've coached, consider leaving their careers. For some of us, it is a very deliberate lifestyle choice that suits our needs and values. For others, the reasons are less positive. In some cases an unrealistic or extreme desire to overachieve results in disappointment. (If I can't live up to my high expectations at work, I'll stay home.) In other cases, a failure to prioritize tasks may mean that we are simply spread too thin. Finally, sometimes it is a lack of support at home and work, which causes us to burn out and give up on our careers.

One of our coaches worked with Jeanne, a management consultant living in a rural community out West. Jeanne made the long commute every week to Manhattan to see her lead client. She flew out on Sunday afternoon and returned back home on Thursday night. It was a bit of a grind, but Jeanne loved her job. And the routine worked out fine until her husband, after years of planning, achieved his dream of opening his own restaurant.

His working hours included Friday through Sunday brunch, but by Sunday afternoons, Jeanne was leaving for the airport, headed for New York again. Suddenly they had opposing schedules—and never saw each other.

Jeanne made it work for several months, but the perks of her job were quickly overshadowed by the strain it was putting on her marriage. Jeanne could see only one option. She put together her resignation letter and planned to quit when she returned from traveling the following week. Before she handed in her resignation, Jeanne called her coach to give her a heads-up.

Diane, her coach, asked what it would take for her to continue working, and whether she'd talked with her employer about it. Jeanne replied that it would require the flexibility to fly out late Monday mornings instead of Sunday afternoon so that she could spend Sunday night and Monday morning with her husband. And, no, she hadn't had this conversation with anyone. Until Diane mentioned it, she hadn't even planned to ask.

Jeanne worked up the courage to ask her manager if she could possibly fly out on Monday afternoon instead of Sunday afternoon. He replied, "Of course, Jeanne, do whatever you need to do."

Stressful situations have a way of causing us to make extreme decisions that we might later regret. Jeanne was thrilled to keep her job. She had been twelve hours away from leaving behind a great career, and it took only one quick conversation to solve her problem.

The highly publicized 2003 *New York Times Magazine* article by Lisa Belkin, who coined the phrase "the opt-out revolution," argued that mothers were choosing to stay at home in greater numbers because the pressure of balancing work and family was so intense.[9] The argument was later challenged with the assertion that a more pressing reason women opt out is that today's companies are not appropriately structured to allow working mothers to succeed. A study from the Center for WorkLife Law, for example, argued that "inflexible, all-or-nothing workplaces drive women out of breadwinner roles and men out of caregiver roles. The result is many fathers working longer hours than they would like and many mothers working fewer hours than they would like."[10]

Although we can't control all of the systemic realities that create an uphill climb for women, we can stand together and look for creative solutions that will help us have the lives and careers we want. There's clearly nothing wrong with making the choice to put a career on hold as a part of your bigger plan. However, as both Jeanne and Kathryn learned, it helps to put the situation in perspective.

Your Turn . . .

Once more, please take a moment to answer a few questions.

How would you characterize your comfort level with ambiguity?

Do you consider yourself to be a positive thinker?

Do you have an upbeat perspective on your accomplishments?

What are some ways in which you blend your career and your life?

What is the story you tell yourself about why it's all or nothing?

The New Rule: It's Both-And

In our interview with Bonnie St. John, Olympic champion, motivational speaker, and author of *Live Your Joy,* she tells us about an "aha" moment: "For me, the epiphany was that it doesn't need to be a teeter-totter. I avoid the extreme ups and downs and guilt. Instead, it's what I call blending." By "blending," St. John means that she has created a life that brings work and family aspirations together in a fluid way. It allows for personal satisfaction and control. St. John looks for creative solutions to accomplishing her goals, but she's not doing every little thing herself—only the important things. She goes on to say, "With blending there is a possibility of having more of both. It isn't simple, it isn't trivial, but it is possible."

What we love about St. John's perspective is that she's found a smart, holistic way to think about her world—one that allows her to live into her goals without making herself crazy. She's breaking her own rules and creating new ones that work for her.

THE NEW RULES

1. Don't limit yourself.

2. Just get over it.

3. Be an entrepreneur.

4. Get centered.

5. Call in reinforcements.

Don't Limit Yourself

Adopting a Both-And mind-set requires us to break away from negative and extreme thinking. Research tells us that having a positive outlook lowers anxiety and actually increases lifespan. Not only that, optimists have better coping skills when the going gets tough.[11]

In our coaching work, we've found that it takes effort and commitment to rid ourselves of negative thoughts. The first step is identifying that you are prone to extreme or negative thoughts. Not all of us are natural optimists, but it's something we can work on. The next step is remembering to correct yourself in real time—question your negative thoughts as they occur, and determine if they are valid or a result of cognitive distortions.

If this is hitting home for you, take a look at Martin Seligman's book *Authentic Happiness*.[12] Read it and take his advice. Seligman's work in the new science of positive psychology suggests ways to be more of an optimist, be more positive and hopeful in your outlook, and manage your negative thinking. In short, with practice, natural pessimists can learn to be optimists!

Beyond dispelling negativity, another way to change our mind-set for the better is to practice integrative thinking. Roger Martin, dean of the Rotman School of Management, argues that the best leaders today are able to "hold two conflicting ideas in constructive tension."[13] This practice is diametrically opposed to all-or-nothing extremes. The ability to consider opposing ideas simultaneously helps us find creative solutions to complex problems. According to Martin, integrative thinkers search for creative resolutions of tensions, rather than accepting unpleasant trade-offs; they keep the entire problem in mind while working on its individual pieces; and they take a broader view of what is salient.[14]

In his book *The Opposable Mind,* Martin offers examples of integrative thinking: "Nandan Nilekani, the builder and CEO of what is perhaps India's most successful global IT powerhouse, Infosys Technologies Limited, says that when he's confronted with two fundamentally opposed sets of requirements, his first inclination is to ask, 'Are there solutions that satisfy both?' And when asked whether he thought strategy or execution was more important, Jack Welch, the former chairman and CEO of General Electric, responded, 'I don't think it's an either-or.'"[15]

Just Get Over It

We've found that women prefer everything to proceed along smoothly; we are more bothered than men by the little bumps in the road. Although it is easier said than done, sometimes we'd be a lot happier if we simply decided to let go of the little things that don't amount to much.

One way the desire to maintain perfect order manifests itself at work is in our need to close the loop on everything. Many times, even when a woman is promoted, she continues to finish the assignments associated with her old role. *I don't want to disappoint my team,* they say. Or *People are counting on me to finish this up.* Give this a try: let it go.

A friend of Mary's has a college-age daughter, Bree, who has a breezy way of waving a finger through air in an arc as she says to her mother, *Mom, just get over it!* Are there things you can *just get over?*

Be an Entrepreneur

Being able to adapt to adversity and thrive in ambiguous, uncertain situations has become a primary career survival skill. Change, as they say, is the new normal. Paradoxically, many organizations themselves are ill-equipped or poorly structured to deal with uncertainty; they require consistent and reliable results in order to please shareholders, but still want a nimble and innovative workforce.

Given these challenges, we find ourselves coaching women to have an entrepreneurial perspective. Even in a big-business setting, being an entrepreneur opens you up to a world of possibilities. Here's how you can think like one:

Be nimble. An uncertain world requires a willingness to experiment. By "nimble," we mean being open to new ideas and ready to respond if an opportunity emerges. The changes occurring in most industries require this agile, entrepreneurial perspective. The desire to gravitate toward what's new may seem like a personality trait one is born with, but putting yourself in new situations gets easier with practice.

Be innovative. Innovation is another tool of choice for harnessing new opportunities in an environment where the outcome is highly uncertain. People who can spot trends and see beyond the obvious context are the ones who—along with the lucky organizations for which they work—will be in a position to benefit from uncertainty. Look for a novel way of doing something or bring an idea from another industry and use it in your own. eBay, for example, was born when cofounders Pierre Omidyar and Jeff Skoll decided to take the idea of a garage sale and bring it online to create the first Internet auction site.

Be optimistic. Out of fear of the unknown, many of us try to hide from change and uncertainty. A great way to mitigate our fear is to look at the upside of the situation. Turn it around and see what opportunities you find. Entrepreneurs are natural bootstrappers; they look for ways to make things work on lean budgets.

Regardless of whether you are naturally oriented toward uncertainty, having an open and entrepreneurial mind-set offers benefits for anyone in business. Although life's uncertainties are largely beyond our control, simply scanning the horizon for signs of change will make you more ready to face it when it occurs.

Get Centered

Maintaining a satisfying work-life balance sometimes feels like a hopeless struggle. But even if genuine work-life balance is a big fat myth, the kind of balance we're talking about is emotional—being on an even keel and having a handle on the priorities in your life. You're feeling challenged at work but not pulling your hair out. The kids made it to school with matching socks and lunch money. You (almost) made it to yoga this week. Like Bonnie St. John, think of it as blending, not balancing.

A life in sync will look different for each one of us, but there are ways you can help yourself get there. Here's what we suggest:

Take baby steps. There's nothing like actively taking charge of a problem to make you feel empowered. If something isn't working—people aren't answering your emails, your hairstyle is bothering you, your smart phone is eating your text messages, whatever—try something else. Nothing major; just take baby steps. Be agile. Continue to tinker with your routine until you solve the problem. It's a simple way to incrementally improve your day every day.

Make a case for what you need. If you want or need a level of work flexibility that's beyond the organizational norm, step up and present a business case. If rearranging your work schedule means you'll be more productive and less stressed, chances are you'll make a persuasive case. And embarking on an analysis and proposal, after all, demonstrates that you've taken the time to consider the challenges as well as upside for you and the organization.

Take time to think. Schedule some regular time for *yourself* —go for a run, take a class, do some gardening, meet a friend. Do whatever helps you recharge and reflect. Allowing yourself to reserve this little bit of personal space will help you clear your mind for more strategic thinking.

In addition to taking a little breather, spending time away from your staff and email is practically required once you reach a certain level in your career. Getting out from behind your desk and enjoying a change of scenery help you do what you are paid for—think ... about the big picture, about strategy, and about ways to improve and innovate.

Call In Reinforcements

One of the great things about being human is that there are more than six-and-a-half billion people having some of the same experiences as you. So why try to figure everything out all on your own? Having a solid support network is a prerequisite not only for career success but also for maintaining that blending of work and home that allows you to have a well-rounded life.

Start by finding support at work. As we've discussed, it's vital to recruit sponsors who will help pave the way for your career opportunities within the organization. We also recommend assembling a group of supporters who will make up your personal board of directors. Beyond these mentoring roles, it's just as important to surround yourself with a few trusted peers—professional friends who complete your support network at work. These are individuals to whom you have a personal connection. They have your back in a crisis, and you have their ears when you need to vent, share a war story, or ask for advice. Also make sure you have support at home. Your spouse, friends, and family serve the same function on the personal front. They not only offer moral, emotional, and financial support but also pick up the slack when necessary.

Finally, reach out and support the women around you. It goes without saying that you'll support your family. But it is also your responsibility to reciprocate at work by supporting and mentoring other women who are making their way up in your organization. Although there has been some press and even some research that supports the notion that women don't advocate for each other, our experience tells us that great things happen when women step up to support other women.

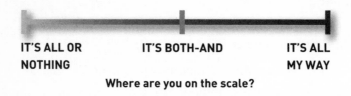

| IT'S ALL OR | IT'S BOTH-AND | IT'S ALL |
| NOTHING | | MY WAY |

Where are you on the scale?

Are you an all-or-nothing thinker, or can you keep things in perspective? We're asking you to look for solutions that are not always obvious or perfect. We women (more often than men) have to make tough choices that result in feelings of guilt—whether relating to family or to work or both. We need to stand up, stand together, and own our choices. We know as well as you that guilt comes with the territory.

Gail Evans told us, "I had a really smart question from a woman whom I was coaching recently. She said to me, 'When are we women going to stop whining about our lack of work-life balance and start fighting for a seat at the table where we will have the power to address these issues?' That's an important way of saying it. We spend a lot of time fixated on balance that does not exist and feeling guilty about the time we spend working. Somehow, we're still waiting for permission to succeed."

These are the New Rules we have created to help you get started. *What New Rules do you need to create for yourself?*

EXECUTIVE SUMMARY

1. Although extreme behavior, such as perfectionism, can be a conduit for ambition, studies indicate that it also leads to dissatisfaction and burnout. Striving for perfection is not only hard on us as individuals; it can also have a negative impact on our performance as leaders.

2. The Old Rules say, *I'm prone to negative thinking; everything is black and white; success means doing it all;* and *I'll opt out.* These are the rules to break.

3. Adopting a Both-And mind-set requires us to break away from negative and extreme thinking. Positive psychology (Martin Seligman) and integrative thinking (an approach pioneered by Roger Martin) offer clues on how to break away from inflexible thinking.

4. Opting out of a career is just one response to an overburdened life. Before making this momentous move, you should revisit your life plan and your personal support system.

5. Borrowing some of the attributes of an entrepreneur — agility, innovation, and optimism — allows us to manage amid uncertainty.

6. Take some time out on a regular basis. Do whatever helps you recharge and reflect. Allowing yourself to reserve this little bit of personal space will help you clear your mind for strategic thinking.

9

STAND TOGETHER AND CLOSE RANKS

The future belongs to those who believe in the beauty of their dreams.
—ELEANOR ROOSEVELT

We've told you our big dream: we want to see women make up at least 30 percent of the leaders at the top levels of corporate America within the next ten years. We believe that 30 percent will be a tipping point for change—a change that will be positive not just for women but for everyone.

Ann Moore, former chairman of Time Inc., put it this way: "Business is better with women in it. We add real value in terms of results and in terms of our leadership style. Women have a different definition of success. The corporate model doesn't always satisfy us, so we drop out or go into small business. In some ways that's too bad, because big business will be better when we have more women leaders."

Let's review what we know. We're good for the bottom line. The research firm Catalyst studied 353 Fortune 500 companies and found that those with more women serving as senior leaders had significantly higher returns on equity.[1] Women are natural consensus builders and emotionally intelligent collaborators; we're well suited for the emerging, less hierarchical workplace of the future.[2] Our gains in educational attainment have significantly outpaced those of men. We have higher graduation rates at all academic levels, and more women than men earn college degrees.[3] Finally, we have tremendous spending power. According to she-conomy.com, 85 percent of all consumer purchases are made by women, including homes, new cars, and health care.[4]

But despite all the good news and steady progress, we're a long way from achieving equal leadership representation at the most senior ranks. We believe that to get red suits at the table, women must stand together and be the drivers of change at three levels: we need individual, group, and systemic change.

Individual Level: Awareness, Choice, Then Change

We work with women every day to encourage them to break their own rules. Our framework for change at the individual level consists of three phases: awareness, choice, then change.

Awareness

Good leaders are self-aware—they have an accurate understanding of their strengths and weaknesses, their accomplishments and needs. But in an opaque corporate environment, gaining a handle on where we stand professionally is tricky.

A few years back, Jill was working with a global bank to determine why so few women were succeeding in senior roles. Women made their way in, but then stalled—or sometimes completely flamed out—once they reached upper management status.

Jill spent some time interviewing five members of the executive committee. What she heard floored her: the male leaders weren't giving their female colleagues honest feedback. Even when they witnessed a major problem or performance issue, they were keeping it to themselves. Here's what they said:

"She wasn't playing the game right, but I was afraid she would cry
    if I told her how she was being perceived."
"Every time I offered her direction, she asked question after question.
    I wasn't getting anywhere. She is too 'high maintenance.'"
"I was afraid the diversity police would get me if I told her the
    truth."
"I wasn't going to draw her a picture. That's not the way we do
    things around here. She needs to figure it out on her own."

These guys were basically letting the women drive off a cliff! In fairness to the gentlemen, they weren't being malicious or calculating. In fact, they were just doing what came naturally. The culture of the bank was casual, and the feedback loop was very informal. Performance reviews were not very highly structured for the senior-most managers.

Jill observed how men in this company offered feedback to each other and saw that it was off the cuff. After a major presentation, for example, two men walked out of the meeting together, each eyeballing their BlackBerrys. Without looking up, one said to the other, "Hey, man, don't do the close like that next time—it didn't work." The other guy replied, "Okay." That was the sum total of their exchange.

We're not saying that all companies are opposed to direct feedback, only that men and women communicate very differently. You may be waiting for explicit guidance that will never materialize.

In addition to being attuned to the culture of your company, there are other ways to make sure you are aware of your development needs and to know where you stand in the organization. Relying on your trusted network is one way. Have a few savvy colleagues to whom you can turn for the truth. Ask the tough questions and be ready to reciprocate if they need your objective guidance. Use your sponsor and your personal board of directors, as we discussed earlier in the book.

Expert assistance—such as professional coaching—is another smart option for executives. Women are quick studies, so targeted advice will have an enormous impact. The one-on-one assessment, videotaping, and 360° feedback organized by a trained professional will give you very specific information as well as an infusion of confidence. Finally, solicit feedback from your manager, but be politically savvy enough to remain calm when it is negative. See it for what it is: an opportunity for change.

Choice

Once you have gathered enough information to see how you are being perceived, you have an opportunity for change. It's up to you to make the move. Change requires a decision. You can decide to change or stay the same. We ask our clients, *Are you all in or all out?* Actually making the decision to change is a powerful act.

According to Marshall Goldsmith, "Successful people have an intense need for self-determination. They believe they do what they do because they have made a choice—not because they have to do it! The more successful someone is, the more likely this is the case. These two characteristics are connected. When we do what we choose to do, we're more committed to it and enthusiastic about it."[5]

Change

Once you have decided to make a change, put together a plan for yourself. Use the advice in this book as a guide as you break and rewrite your personal rules for career success. The self-assessment questions in each of the preceding chapters will help get you started. Change requires not only reflection but also deliberate practice.

Here's what Ann Moore, recently retired CEO of Time Inc., told us: "I always tell people to look at their career like a dance card. If you fill out the dance card, ultimately you will get where you need to go, because you will in the end have the skills and the experience you need to get the job that you want."

Are there specific items you need to add to your dance card?

Group Level: Women Supporting Other Women

"There's a place in Hell reserved for women who don't help other women."

—Madeleine Albright

We are passionate believers in the idea that women must help other women succeed. In our interview with Gail Evans, former CNN executive and author of *Play Like a Man, Win Like a Woman,* she put it this way: "We need to push each other up. The guys push each other up all the time. And if they don't succeed, they just slap each other on the back and say *It was a good try; we'll go for it next time.* We have to do the same—we must surround ourselves with supportive women who will give us a boost."

There is a common belief that women would rather tear each other down than build each other up. But is it true that we're jealous and reluctant to be supportive, or is it all just a story line on reality TV? According to the Workplace Bullying Institute, negative and disruptive behavior at work is not gender dependent; organizational culture is a better predictor than gender. It goes on to say that a culture that carries no accountability paves the way for interpersonal dysfunction.[6]

Some experts assert that because the workplace is male dominated, women often feel the need to compete against one another for fewer opportunities, thus creating an atmosphere of jealously and resentment.[7] But even if this is a legitimate twist in the double-bind quagmire that women face, we nonetheless need to start playing together and stop making our career success a solo sport.

There are two levels of group support we can and must provide each other if we are to pave a path to power for women: standing together and closing ranks.

The first level of support, standing together, is simply about giving other women sincere moral support and genuine assistance: pulling for each other, networking, and lending each other a hand.

Gail Evans told us this story about women supporting women:

I was giving a speech recently when a woman stood up and said, very earnestly: "I don't work right now because I have little children. I go to the elementary school every day to pick up my kids, and the same child is left waiting for a ride every afternoon. His mother has a big career. Some days that child is picked up by a neighbor and some days by a taxi service. I think that's terrible. I don't see why women working is a positive thing for children." So I said, "You live a few blocks away from that woman. Why don't you call her and volunteer to drive her son home from school a few days a week? Help her out and see what happens. Seven or eight years from now, when you are ready to go back to work and that woman is the senior vice president at GM, you pick up the phone again. Ask her for help with your resume or to introduce you to someone in HR. What do you think she's going to say?" We're all in this together. We can help each other.

From what we see every day in our work, plenty of women understand the need to stand together. Ann Moore told us of one such experience: "When I became chairman of Time Inc., Governor Ann Richards came in to see me and said, 'I'm here to teach you to play at the varsity level.' And she was the best. If there was anything ever written in the *New York Post* or a blog about me, she would always send me a little note and say 'Just plow ahead, girl.' I will never forget that."

A second way that women can support women is by closing ranks. This is true solidarity: women promoting other women. When a position opens up at the senior level, women need to support one of their own to be chosen for the job. We need to support each other, even if it means we have to wait in line longer for our own turn.

We saw an example of this at a client of ours, a midsize manufacturing company. There was a position open on the executive committee and several qualified candidates. Two leading candidates were women; several others were men. The two women saw that by competing with each other, their chances for advancement were slim. So they made a choice. They united to create a strong coalition of support around one of them—and she was elevated onto the executive committee.

There is so much we can accomplish if we stand together and close ranks.

System-Level Support

Building a business infrastructure and a society that support our ambition and allow us a less arduous path to success takes time—but it will happen. It will happen because we will refuse to allow circumstances to remain the same. Our relentless networking and political savvy will open doors. Our support of each other will create networks of mentors and active sponsors. Our collaborative leadership style and emotional intelligence will make us more relevant in a networked world. Our growing confidence will compensate for the double standards and double binds that keep us in supporting roles. Our time in the leadership pipeline will offer us experience and access to important and visible assignments. We will rise to senior leadership levels.

Helen Mets-Morris, vice president and general manager at Avery Dennison, put it this way: "Breaking through is a huge cultural challenge. But I am so much more effective now that I'm aware of the size of the challenge. In terms of motivation, I believe that every one of us who is working for change is making a difference."

Concluding Words on Change

At its heart, this is a book about driving change: making individual, group, and systemic progress. On a personal level, resisting change is a common defense mechanism that can hold each of us back—from new experiences, from breakthrough insights, and from career success. On a group level, women not supporting other women will hold back progress for all of us. On an organizational level, resisting change can be lethal. Perhaps that's why change management has become an entire cottage industry in business consulting. But even if you know you need to evolve and change and have a legion of experts guiding you through, the prospect of actually changing can still be intimidating.

There is a mountain of research that explains the biological and psychological reasons why people avoid change and stay stuck in bad situations. In their book, *Leadership on the Line,* Ronald Heifetz and Marty Linsky say that "habits, values, and attitudes, even dysfunctional ones, are part of one's identity. To change the way people see and do things is to challenge how they define themselves."[8]

Challenging how we define ourselves is a tall order. Throughout this book, we've asked you to examine your individual thought patterns and to change the way you think about success. That takes work. But even if you struggle with change, the truth is that once you take that leap, you'll be rewarded. We've found that when the women we work with make even small changes, they feel brave and invigorated. We tell them to remember those feelings—they make change a little bit easier the next time.

NOTES

Chapter 1: Our Vision

1. Lois Joy, Nancy M. Carter, Harvey M. Wagner, and Sriram Wagner, *The Bottom Line: Corporate Performance and Women's Representation on Boards*, Catalyst report, October 2007, www.catalyst.org/publication/200/the-bottom-line-corporate-performance-and-womens-representation-on-boards; McKinsey & Company, "Women Matter: Gender Diversity, a Corporate Performance Driver," 2007, www.mckinsey.com/careers/women/social_sector_impact/~/media/Reports/Women/Mckinsey_women_matter.ashx.

2. "Women CEOs," *Fortune,* CNNMoney.com, May 3, 2010, http://money.cnn.com/magazines/fortune/fortune500/2010/womenceos/.

3. Catalyst, "U.S. Labor Force, Population, and Education," March 2010, www.catalyst.org/publication/202/us-labor-force-population-and-education.

4. U.S. Department of Labor, U.S. Bureau of Labor Statistics, *Highlights of Women's Earnings in 2008,* Report 1017, July 2009, www.bls.gov/cps/cpswom2008.pdf.

5. Deloitte, "Women's Initiative Annual Report," www.deloitte.com/view/en_US/us/About/Womens-Initiative/3e68e8e99defd110VgnVCM100000ba42f00aRCRD.htm.

6. Deloitte, "Women's Initiative Annual Report," cited in Joy and others, *The Bottom Line.*

7. Cristian L. Dezsö and David Gaddis Ross, *"Girl Power: Female Participation in Top Management and Firm Performance,"* research paper no. RHS 06–104 (University of Maryland, 2008).

8. Roy D. Adler, *Women in the Executive Suite Correlate to High Profits,* 2001, www.csripraktiken.se/wp-content/uploads/adler_web.pdf.

9. Sylvia Ann Hewlett, "Are Your Best Female Employees a Flight Risk?" (blog post), October 5, 2009, http://blogs.hbr.org/hbr/hewlett/2009/10/smart_women_stronger _companies.html.

10. The Conference Board of Canada, *Women on Boards Not Just the Right Thing ... but the "Bright" Thing*, May 2002, www.europeanpwn.net/files/women_on_boards _canada.pdf.

11. Catalyst, *The Double-Bind Dilemma for Women in Leadership: Damned If You Do, Doomed If You Don't*, 2007, www.catalyst.org/file/45/the%20double-bind%20dilemma%20for%20women%20in%20leadership%20damned%20if %20you%20do,%20doomed%20if%20you%20don't.pdf.

Chapter 2: Break Your Own Rules

1. Marshall Goldsmith with Mark Reiter, *What Got You Here Won't Get You There: How Successful People Become Even More Successful* (New York: Hyperion, 2007).

Chapter 3: Take Center Stage

1. Emiliana R. Simon-Thomas, "Are Women More Empathic Than Men?" *Greater Good*, Summer 2007, http://greatergood.berkeley.edu/article/item/women_more _empathic_than_men/.

2. K. V. Petrides, Adrian Furnham, and G. Neil Martin, "Estimates of Emotional and Psychometric Intelligence: Evidence for Gender-Based Stereotypes," *Journal of Social Psychology* 144 (2004): 149–162.

3. Brian Alexander, "Women Guilty of Feeling Too Guilty, Study Shows," March 11, 2010, www.msnbc.msn.com/id/35788411/ns/health-sexual_health/.

4. Carol L. Martin, Caroline H. Wood, and Jane K. Little, "The Development of Gender Stereotype Components," *Child Development* 61 (1990): 1891–1904; Susan D. Witt, "Parental Influence on Children's Socialization to Gender Roles," *Adolescence* 32 (Summer 1997): 253–259.

5. Marsha Weinraub, Lynda P. Clemens, Alan Sockloff, Theresa Ethridge, Edward Gracely, and Barbara Myers, "The Development of Sex Role Stereotypes in the Third Year: Relationships to Gender Labeling, Gender Identity, Sex-Typed Toy Preferences, and Family Characteristics," *Child Development* 55 (1984): 1493–1503.

Chapter 4: Proceed Until Apprehended

1. Linda Babcock, "Women, Repeat This: Don't Ask, Don't Get," *New York Times*, April 6, 2008, www.nytimes.com/2008/04/06/jobs/06pre.html.

2. Diane Reay, "Spice Girls, 'Nice Girls,' 'Girlies' and Tomboys: Gender Discourses, Girls' Cultures and Femininities in the Primary Classroom," *Gender and Education* 13, no. 2 (2001): 153–166.

3. Anna Fels, "Do Women Lack Ambition?" *Harvard Business Review*, April 2004, http://hbr.org/product/do-women-lack-ambition/an/R0404B-PDF-ENG; see also Anna Fels, *Necessary Dreams: Ambition in Women's Changing Lives* (New York: Pantheon, 2004).

4. Fels, "Do Women Lack Ambition?"

5. Linda Babcock and Sara Laschever, *Women Don't Ask: Negotiation and the Gender Divide* (Princeton, NJ: Princeton University Press, 2003).

6. Fels, *Necessary Dreams*, xvii, 5.

Chapter 5: Project Personal Power

1. Alice Eagly and Linda Carli, *Through the Labyrinth: The Truth About How Women Become Leaders* (Boston: Harvard Business School Press, 2007), 104–105.

2. Sandra Ford Walston, "Women Integrating Workday Courage," *Women in Business* 54, no. 2 (2002): 28–29.

3. Linda Babcock and Sara Laschever, *Women Don't Ask: Negotiation and the Gender Divide* (Princeton, NJ: Princeton University Press, 2003).

4. Babcock and Laschever, *Women Don't Ask*.

5. Pauline Rose Clance and Suzanne Ament Imes, "The Impostor Phenomenon Among High Achieving Women: Dynamics and Therapeutic Intervention," *Psychotherapy Theory, Research and Practice* 15, no. 3 (1978): 241–247.

6. Susan Pinker, *The Sexual Paradox: Troubled Boys, Gifted Girls and the Real Difference Between the Sexes* (New York: Scribner, 2008).

7. Satoshi Kanazawa and Kaja Perina, "Why Do So Many Women Experience the 'Imposter Syndrome'?" *Scientific Fundamentalist* (blog), December 13, 2009, www.psychologytoday.com/blog/the-scientific-fundamentalist/200912/why-do-so-many-women-experience-the-imposter-syndrome.

8. Ibid.

9. Deborah Tannen, *You Just Don't Understand: Men and Women in Conversation* (New York: Morrow, 1990), 331.

10. Ibid., 332.

11. Babcock and Laschever, *Women Don't Ask*, 6.

12. Robin L. Pinkley and Robin B. Northcraft, *Get Paid What You're Worth* (New York: St. Martin's Press, 2000), 169, cited in Babcock and Laschever, *Women Don't Ask*, 7.

13. Clance and Imes, "The Impostor Phenomenon."

14. Ibid., 2.

15. Marjorie Brody (www.brodypro.com) is the author of six books, including *Career Magic: A Women's Guide to Reward and Recognition.*

16. Many people have studied the idea of confidence markers, including Anne E. Beall, Alan Nelson, Chip Heath, Dan Heath, Camille Lavington, C. L. Ridgeway, Deborah Tannen, Harrison Monarth, Larina Kase, Jo-Ellan Dimitrius, Mark Mazzarella, Julius Fast, Norma Carr-Ruffino, Rich Brandon, Marty Seldman, Sonya Hamlin, and Victoria A. Seitz.

Chapter 6: Be Politically Savvy

1. Quoted in Polly Labarre, "The New Face of Office Politics," *Fast Company*, September 30, 1999, www.fastcompany.com/magazine/28/newface.html.

2. Ibid.

3. Women in Technology, "Female IT Workers 'Concerned over Office Politics,' " February 4, 2008, www.womenintechnology.co.uk/news/female-it-workers--concerned-over-office-politics--news-18532857.

4. Lois P. Frankel, *Nice Girls Don't Get the Corner Office: 101 Unconscious Mistakes Women Make That Sabotage Their Careers* (New York: Warner Business Books, 2004).

5. Kathleen Kelley Reardon, "Using Office Politics to Your Advantage," womens-media.com, October 4, 2003, www.womensmedia.com/work/185-using-office-politics-to-your-advantage.html.

6. Carol F. Gilligan, *In a Different Voice: Psychological Theory and Women's Development* (Cambridge: Harvard University Press, 1982).

7. Kathleen Kelley Reardon, *The Secret Handshake: Mastering the Politics of the Business Inner Circle* (New York: Currency/Doubleday, 2001), 192–193.

8. Labarre, "The New Face of Office Politics."

9. "Female Heads of State and Government Currently in Office," *Worldwide Guide to Women in Leadership*, www.guide2womenleaders.com/Current-Women-Leaders.htm.

10. "Current Female Heads of State and Government," *Worldwide Guide to Women in Leadership*, www.guide2womenleaders.com/index.html.

11. Rich Morin and D'Vera Cohn, "Women Call the Shots at Home; Public Mixed on Gender Roles in Jobs," Pew Research Center, September 25, 2008, http://pewresearch.org/pubs/967/gender-power.

12. Herminia Ibarra, Nancy M. Carter, and Christine Silva, "Why Men Still Get More Promotions Than Women," *Harvard Business Review,* November 2010, http://hbr.org/2010/09/why-men-still-get-more-promotions-than-women/sb3.

13. "Paving the Way; Sharon Allen: From Boise to the Boardroom," *California CPA,* CBS MoneyWatch.com, October 2005, http://findarticles.com/p/articles/mi_m0ICC/is_4_74/ai_n15763056/pg_3/?tag=content;col1.

14. Kathryn Mayer, "Gender and Office Politics: Do Women and Organizational Politics Mix?" *Political Savvy,* www.politicalsavvy.com/docs/genderandpolitics.html.

Chapter 7: Play to Win

1. Vipin Gupta, Sylvia Maxfield, Mary Shapiro, and Susan Hass, "Risky Business: Busting the Myth of Women as Risk Averse," CGO Insight briefing note 28, Center for Gender in Organizations, Simmons School of Management, 2009, www.simmons.edu/som/docs/insights_28.pdf.

2. "Women Business Leaders Are Risk-Takers: Survey Debunks Gender Myth," Simmons press release, May 7, 2009, www.simmons.edu/overview/about/news/press/820.php.

3. Ibid.

4. Herminia Ibarra, "Women and the 'Vision Thing,' " *INSEAD Knowledge,* February 2009, http://knowledge.insead.edu/WomenandVision.cfm?vid=181.

5. Herminia Ibarra and Otilia Obodaru, "Women and the Vision Thing," *Harvard Business Review*, January 2009. http://hbr.org/2009/01/women-and-the-vision-thing/ib.

6. Deepali Bagati and Nancy M. Carter, *Leadership Gender Gap in India Inc.: Myths and Realities,* 2010, www.catalyst.org/file/408/leadership_gender_gap_in_india-final.pdf.

7. "The Women Who Want to Run the World," *Newsweek,* August 27, 2010, www.newsweek.com/2010/08/27/chinese-women-are-more-ambitious-than-americans.html.

8. Pat Heim, *Hardball for Women: Winning at the Game of Business* (New York: Plume, 2005), 15–16.

9. Timothy Butler, *Getting Unstuck: How Dead Ends Become New Paths* (Boston: Harvard Business Press, 2007), xv–xvi.

10. Herminia Ibarra, *Working Identity: Unconventional Strategies for Reinventing Your Career* (Boston: Harvard Business School Press, 2003).

11. Julie Morgenstern, *Never Check Email in the Morning,* (New York: Simon & Schuster, 2004), 72–76.

Chapter 8: It's Both-And

1. "Perfectionism Hits Working Women," *BBC News,* May 28, 2009, http://news .bbc.co.uk/2/hi/8072739.stm.

2. Jacqueline K. Mitchelson, "Seeking the Perfect Balance: Perfectionism and Work-Family Conflict," *Journal of Occupational and Organizational Psychology* 82, no. 2 (June 2009): 349–367.

3. James Allan Davis, Tom W. Smith, and Peter V. Marsden, *General Social Surveys, 1972–2008: Cumulative Codebook* (Chicago: National Opinion Research Center, 2009) (National Data Program for the Social Sciences Series, no. 18).

4. Marcus Buckingham, *Find Your Strongest Life: What the Happiest and Most Successful Women Do Differently* (Nashville, TN: Thomas Nelson, 2009), 154.

5. Melissa Jackson, "Why Perfect Is Not Always Best," June 19, 2004, http://news .bbc.co.uk/2/hi/health/3815479.stm.

6. David D. Burns, *The Feeling Good Handbook* (New York: Morrow, 1989).

7. Genie Z. Laborde, *Influencing with Integrity: Management Skills for Communication and Negotiation* (Palo Alto, CA: Syntony, 1984), 2.

8. Joann Loviglio, "Steinem: Notion of Women 'Having It All' Is a Myth," *boston .com,* November 12, 2010, www.boston.com/news/nation/articles/2010/11/12/ steinem_notion_of_women_having_it_all_is_a_myth/?rss_id=Boston.com+— +Latest+news.

9. Lisa Belkin, "The Opt-Out Revolution," *New York Times Magazine,* October 26, 2003, www.nytimes.com/2003/10/26/magazine/26WOMEN.html?pagewanted =all.

10. Joan C. Williams, Jessica Manvell, and Stephanie Bornstein, *"Opt Out" or Pushed Out? How the Press Covers Work/Family Conflict—the Untold Story of Why Women Leave the Workforce,* Center for WorkLife Law, UC Hastings College of Law, 2006, www.worklifelaw.org/pubs/OptOutPushedOut.pdf.

11. Beverly H. Brummett and others, "Prediction of All-Cause Mortality by the Minnesota Multiphasic Personality Inventory Optimism-Pessimism Scale Scores: Study of a College Sample During a 40-Year Follow-up Period," *Mayo Clinic Proceedings* 81, no. 12 (2006): 1541–1544.

12. Martin E. P. Seligman, *Authentic Happiness: Using the New Positive Psychology to Realize Your Potential for Lasting Fulfillment* (New York: Free Press, 2003).

13. Roger L. Martin, *The Opposable Mind* (Boston: Harvard Business School Press, 2007), 7.

14. Martin, *Opposable Mind.*

15. Ibid., 105, 114.

Chapter 9: Stand Together and Close Ranks

1. Catalyst, *The Bottom Line: Connecting Corporate Performance and Gender Diversity,* January 2004, www.catalyst.org/file/44/the%20bottom%20line%20connecting %20corporate%20performance%20and%20gender%20diversity.pdf.

2. Claire Shipman and Katty Kay, "Women Will Rule Business," *Time,* May 14, 2009, www.time.com/time/specials/packages/article/0,28804,1898024_1898023 _1898078,00.html.

3. U.S. Department of Commerce Economics and Statistics Administration and Executive Office of the President Office of Management and Budget, *Women in America: Indicators of Social and Economic Well-Being,* March 2011, www.whitehouse.gov/ sites/default/files/rss_viewer/Women_in_America.pdf.

4. The she-conomy.com video is posted on Nicole Crimaldi, "Female Buying Power," Ms. Career Girl, June 13, 2010, www.mscareergirl.com/2010/06/13/female- buying-power/.

5. Marshall Goldsmith, "Choosing to Change," *Bloomberg Businessweek,* May 27, 2008, www.businessweek.com/managing/content/may2008/ca20080527_275979 .htm.

6. Workplace Bullying Institute, "Woman-on-Woman Bullying," May 20, 2009, www.workplacebullying.org/2009/05/20/wow-bullying/.

7. Eve Tahmincioglu, "Women Still Reluctant to Help Each Other," Careers on msnbc.com, www.msnbc.msn.com/id/38060072/ns/business-careers/.

8. Martin Linsky and Ronald A. Heifetz, *Leadership on the Line: Staying Alive Through the Dangers of Leading* (Boston: Harvard Business School Press, 2002), 27.

READING LIST FOR WOMEN LEADERS

Babcock, Linda, and Sara Laschever. *Women Don't Ask: Negotiation and the Gender Divide*. Princeton, NJ: Princeton University Press, 2003.

Barsh, Joanna, Susie Cranston, and Geoffrey Lewis. *How Remarkable Women Lead: The Breakthrough Model for Work and Life*. New York: Crown Business, 2009.

Benko, Cathleen, and Molly Anderson. *The Corporate Lattice: Achieving High Performance in the Changing World of Work*. Boston: Harvard Business Press, 2010.

———, and Anne Weisberg. *Mass Career Customization: Aligning the Workplace with Today's Nontraditional Workforce*. Boston: Harvard Business Press, 2007.

Catalyst. [All reports]. San Francisco: Jossey-Bass.

Evans, Gail. *Play Like a Man, Win Like a Woman*. New York: Broadway Books, 2000.

———. *She Wins, You Win*. New York: Gotham, 2004.

Fels, Anna. *Necessary Dreams: Ambition in Women's Changing Lives*. New York: Pantheon, 2004.

Frankel, Lois P. *Nice Girls Don't Get the Corner Office*. New York: Business Plus, 2004.

Klaus, Peggy. *BRAG! The Art of Tooting Your Own Horn Without Blowing It*. New York: Warner Business Books, 2003.

Lubar, Kathy, and Belle Linda Halpern. *Leadership Presence*. New York: Gotham, 2003.

Tannen, Deborah. *Talking from 9 to 5: Women and Men at Work*. New York: Harper Paperbacks, 1995.

ACKNOWLEDGMENTS

We are deeply grateful to the many people who have supported the three of us as we followed our dream of creating a firm, Flynn Heath Holt Leadership, and writing this book.

To the thousands of exceptional women our firm has coached and trained over the past ten years: you have trusted us and shared your lives with us, and we will never forget you. You are the reason we wrote this book.

To our many friends and colleagues at Deloitte: your firm should win first prize among American businesses! We admire your constant pursuit of excellence in every area, and we especially value what you have done to make your firm an outstanding place for women to succeed.

To our families—mothers, fathers, sisters, brothers, grand-children—but especially to our grown children, Angie, Kate, Taylor, Heath, and David—we are counting on you to use these New Rules to build inclusive work environments for both men and women.

To our consultants and team members at Flynn Heath Holt: thank you for your hard work and the long hours spent to make this book a reality. Special kudos to Vicki Skipper, Townley Moon,

Susan Tracey, Dottie Birch, Chuck Cannon, and John Michael Bishop. You're the best!

To Susan William, our editor at Jossey-Bass: thank you for shining the light on the unique point of view that we bring to this topic.

To Carolyn Monaco, our marketer and agent: you are our spark plug! Thank you for your indefatigable optimism and continuing influence on our book and our business.

To Leslie Stephen, our friend and colleague: thank you for first helping us believe in the possibility of a book.

To Jacqueline Murphy, our collaborator: you are the magician who artfully blended our three voices into one.

ABOUT THE AUTHORS

Jill Flynn, Kathryn Heath, and Mary Davis Holt are nationally recognized experts on women's leadership. Each has commanded senior-level positions in Fortune 100 companies, and each has experienced the hurdles that still face executive women today. Now, as principals of Flynn Heath Holt Leadership (FHHL), they partner with Fortune 1000 companies to customize and implement research-driven development programs that put women into top positions. Their expertise spans the critical areas that drive individual and organizational performance in every sector and at many levels—executive coaching, leadership development, training design, and organizational change. FHHL's clients span industries and include financial services, energy, manufacturing, professional services, nonprofits, and government.

Jill Flynn, M.Ed., specializes in creating and implementing company-specific pipelines for high-potential women. Jill's primary focus is to ensure that every client benefits from new and practical solutions to its leadership challenges—and gets measurable results.

Prior to cofounding FHHL, Jill was senior vice president at the nation's fourth-largest bank, First Union Corporation (later named Wachovia), where she established its leadership development, diversity, organizational consulting, and employee satisfaction initiatives. As the corporation grew exponentially during her tenure, through engaging in dozens of mergers. Jill and her team prepared a cadre of more than one hundred high-potential leaders to assume senior positions; within a three-year time frame, the number of women in these roles increased from 9 percent to 26 percent.

Kathryn Heath, Ph.D., serves as a master executive coach, developer of leadership programs, and training designer. One of the hallmarks of Kathryn's work is addressing organizations' specific business targets through customized programs that move women forward, faster.

Before she cofounded FHHL, Kathryn was senior vice president and director of First University at the nation's fourth-largest bank, First Union Corporation (later named Wachovia), where her inventive and results-focused approach won her numerous awards in the field of learning and development. There, during a period of explosive growth for the bank, Kathryn centralized training, expanded the tools and channels both on-site and remotely, and exponentially increased the training hours per person. She also created programs for high-potential employees—many of whom became the company's topmost leaders.

Mary Davis Holt is an executive coach and keynote speaker on business, women, and leadership. As an in-demand voice, Mary shares her hard-won insights and promotes FHHL's new rules for success to a wide range of audiences.

Prior to joining FHHL, Mary held executive positions at Time Warner, with oversight that included finance, information technology, marketing, human resources, manufacturing, and distribution. She held a number of leadership roles in the publishing group, including senior executive vice president and chief operating officer of Time Life, Inc. Among Mary's many career highlights, she led the management of worldwide manufacturing distribution for all of Time Inc.'s magazines (for example, *Time, Fortune, People,* and *Sports Illustrated*). She also served as president of Time Life Books and Time Life Kids.

Individually, the authors have earned many awards from their business and professional communities. All three actively mentor others and serve on a number of boards.

Together, the authors believe that business is simply better with more women in it—so their mission is to increase the number of women at the top from 11 percent to 30 percent within the next ten years.

Join them today at www.FlynnHeathHolt.com.

INDEX

ABOUT THE AUTHORS' FIRM
Flynn Heath Holt Leadership
Helping Women and Organizations Move Forward, Faster

Flynn Heath Holt is a leadership development and executive coaching firm that specializes in women.

The firm's story likely resonates with your own. Jill Flynn, Kathryn Heath, and Mary Davis Holt excelled in their careers but found that the rules were different at the top. They found themselves asking the hard questions again and again: Why aren't more women in top jobs by now? What's the ROI for retaining women—versus losing them? What does it take for companies to create a pipeline for women who are ready? How can we start having that conversation in our company?

Over time, Jill, Kathryn, and Mary not only found the answers, they achieved senior executive status and made significant contributions to their companies' bottom lines.

 **Jill Flynn** became senior vice president at the nation's fourth largest bank. During her tenure, the bank experienced exponential growth through over 100 mergers—and she established award-winning leadership, diversity, organizational consulting, and employee satisfaction initiatives.

 **Kathryn Heath** became senior vice president at the nation's fourth largest bank. During extraordinary expansion, she spearheaded leadership and management development, centralized worldwide training, and deployed multiple channels for nationwide delivery of new, measurably more effective programs. Kathryn was widely recognized for her inventive and results-focused work.

 **Mary Davis Holt** was senior executive vice president and COO of Time Life, Inc. She also held executive positions at Time Warner with oversight ranging from finance to IT, marketing, and human resources—including worldwide manufacturing for Time Inc.'s magazines including *Time, Fortune, People*, and *Sports Illustrated.*

Now, as partners in their own firm, these outstanding women share a single mission: Sharing their wisdom so that the path to the top is easier for women.

The Authors' Work with Clients

Jill, Kathryn, and Mary believe that leadership drives results, and they have shown their clients that developing and promoting women improves the company's bottom line. Flynn Heath Holt works with Fortune 1000 clients in four practice areas:

→ Keynotes
→ Interactive workshops and seminars
→ Executive coaching
→ Customized development programs

Some clients bring Flynn Heath Holt in to do a workshop. Others request the firm's expertise to create or strengthen a women's initiative for their company. And others need Flynn Heath Holt to implement a program for its high-potential women. Regardless, in every engagement, Flynn Heath Holt's focus is transforming the talent pool to benefit the company's bottom-line.

Learn more by contacting the authors directly at (704) 632-6712 or JFlynn@FlynnHeathHolt.com, KHeath@FlynnHeathHolt.com, or MDHolt@FlynnHeathHolt.com.

www.FlynnHeathHolt.com

A SPECIAL OFFERING
Introduce *Break Your Own Rules* to Your Organization

Authors Jill Flynn, Kathryn Heath, and Mary Davis Holt

- Nationally recognized experts on women's leadership
- Creators of leadership development programs for the Fortune 1000
- Master coaches to executives and to senior teams
- Facilitators of experiential workshops and interactive seminars
- Sought-after keynote speakers

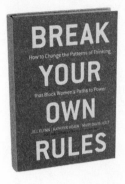